C000001216

1 MONTH OF
FREE
READING

at

www.ForgottenBooks.com

By purchasing this book you are eligible for one month membership to ForgottenBooks.com, giving you unlimited access to our entire collection of over 1,000,000 titles via our web site and mobile apps.

To claim your free month visit:

www.forgottenbooks.com/free958589

ISBN 978-0-260-59754-0
PIBN 10958589

TO THE

EPARTMENT LIBRARY.

JANUARY-MARCH, 1905.

WASHINGTON:
GOVERNMENT PRINTING OFFICE.
1905.

PUBLICATIONS OF THE LIBRARY OF THE DEPARTMENT OF AGRICULTURE.

BULLETINS.

No. 1. Accessions to the Department Library [January–March], 1894.
2. Periodicals and society publications currently received at the Department Library. 1894.
3. Accessions to the Department Library, April–June, 1894.
4. Accessions to the Department Library, July–October, 1894.
5. Accessions to the Department Library, November–December, 1894.
6. Accessions to the Department Library, January–March, 1895.
7. Accessions to the Department Library, April–June, 1895.
8. Accessions to the Department Library, July–September, 1895.
9. List of publications of the U. S. Department of Agriculture from 1841 to June 30, 1895, inclusive. 1896.
10. Accessions to the Department Library, October–December, 1895.
11. Accessions to the Department Library, January–March, 1896.
12. Accessions to the Department Library, April–June, 1896.
13. Accessions to the Department Library, July–September, 1896.
14. Accessions to the Department Library, October–December, 1896.
15. Accessions to the Department Library, January–March, 1897.
16. References to the literature of the sugar beet, exclusive of works in foreign languages; compiled by Claribel R. Barnett. 1897.
17. Accessions to the Department Library, April–June, 1897.
18. Bibliography of poultry; compiled by Emma B. Hawks. 1897.
19. Accessions to the Department Library, July–September, 1897.
20. Reference list of publications relating to edible and poisonous mushrooms; compiled by Josephine A. Clark. 1898.
21. Accessions to the Department Library, October–December, 1897.
22. Accessions to the Department Library, January–March, 1898.
23. Accessions to the Department Library, April–June, 1898.
24. List of publications relating to forestry in the Department Library. 1898.
25. Accessions to the Department Library, July–September, 1898.
26. Accessions to the Department Library, October–December, 1898.
27. Accessions to the Department Library, January–March, 1899.
28. Accessions to the Department Library, April–June, 1899.
29. Accessions to the Department Library, July–September, 1899.
30. Accessions to the Department Library, October–December, 1899.
31. Accessions to the Department Library, January–March, 1900.
32. Accessions to the Department Library, April–June, 1900.
33. Accessions to the Department Library, July–September, 1900.
34. Accessions to the Department Library, October–December, 1900.
35. Accessions to the Department Library, January–March, 1901.
36. Accessions to the Department Library, April–June, 1901.
37. Catalogue of the periodicals and other serial publications (exclusive of U. S. Government publications) in the Library of the U. S. Department of Agriculture; prepared under the direction of Josephine A. Clark, Librarian. 1901.
38. Accessions to the Department Library, July–September, 1901.
39. Accessions to the Department Library, October–December, 1901.
40. Accessions to the Department Library, January–March, 1902.
41. List of references to publications relating to irrigation and land drainage; compiled by Ellen A. Hedrick. 1902.
42. Catalogue of the publications relating to botany in the library of the U. S. Department of Agriculture. 1902.

[Continued on page 3 of cover.]

U. S. DEPARTMENT OF AGRICULTURE.

LIBRARY—BULLETIN No. 54.

JOSEPHINE A. CLARK, Librarian.

ACCESSIONS

TO THE

DEPARTMENT LIBRARY.

JANUARY-MARCH, 1905.

WASHINGTON:

GOVERNMENT PRINTING OFFICE.

1905.

LETTER OF TRANSMITTAL.

U. S. DEPARTMENT OF AGRICULTURE,
OFFICE OF THE LIBRARIAN,
Washington, D. C., April 4, 1905.

SIR: I have the honor to transmit herewith the manuscript of "Accessions to the Department Library, January–March, 1905," and to recommend the publication of the same as Bulletin No. 54 of the Library.

Very respectfully,   JOSEPHINE A. CLARK,
Librarian.

Hon. JAMES WILSON, *Secretary.*

3

CONTENTS.

ACCESSIONS TO THE DEPARTMENT LIBRARY.

JANUARY–MARCH, 1905.

A serial number (e. g., 5—986 or Agr 5—319) following an entry signifies that printed catalogue cards for the book have been issued and are for sale by the Library of Congress. Application should be made to the *Librarian of Congress, Washington, D. C.* (*Card distribution.*)

1. AGRICULTURE.

Argentine Republic—*Agricultura, Ministerio de.* . . . Memoria presentada al honorable congreso por el ministro de agricultura Dr. Wenceslao Escalante, 1903–04. fold. maps in case. 26½ᶜᵐ. Buenos Aires, Talleres de publicaciones de la Oficina meteorológica Argentina, 1904.

——— tomo II anexo A, 1903–04. 26½ᶜᵐ. Buenos Aires, Talleres de publicaciones de la Oficina meteorológica Argentina, 1904.

Arkansas—*Mines, manufactures, and agriculture, Bureau of.* Eighth biennial report . . . for the years 1903 and 1904. illus. 23ᶜᵐ. [n. p., n. d.]

Baldi, Jacinto. . . . Investigación agrícola en la provincia de Catamarca . . . 95 p., 1 l. incl. plates. 5 diagr. 26½ᶜᵐ. Buenos Aires, Compañia Sud-americana de billetes de banco, 1904. (República Argentina. Anales del Ministério de agricultura. Sección agricultura; botánica y agronomía. Agronomía, tomo I, nᵒ. 7.)

Agr 5-319

Bohemia—*Landeskulturrath—Deutsche sektion.* XII. bericht über die tätigkeit . . . im jahre 1903. 27ᶜᵐ. Prag, **V**erlag der Deutschen sektion des Landeskulturrates für das königreich Böhmen, 1904.

Bohemia—*Landeskulturrath—Deutsche sektion.* Zehn jahre landeskultureller arbeit, 1892–1902. Eine uebersicht über die tätigkeit der Deutschen sektion des Landeskulturrates für das königreich Böhmen in den letzten zehn jahren. liv p., 1 l. plates (partly fold.) 27ᶜᵐ. Prag, Im verlag der Deutschen sektion des Landeskulturrates für des königreich Böhmen, 1902.

Burkett, Charles William. Agriculture for beginners; special supplement, by Charles William Burkett, Frank Lincoln Stevens, Daniel Harvey Hill . . . 3 p. l. 58 p. illus. 18½ᶜᵐ. Boston, New York, London [etc.] Ginn & company [1904]

Canada—*Agriculture, Dept. of.* Report of the minister of agriculture . . . for the year ended October 31, 1904. 24½ᶜᵐ. Ottawa, Printed by S. E. Dawson, printer to the king's most excellent Majesty, 1905.

Canada—*Agriculture, Dept. of—Agriculture and dairying, commissioner of.* Evidence of Mr. Jas. W. Robertson . . . before the select standing committee on agriculture and colonization . . . 1897–98, 1903 [pt. 1–3] 25ᶜᵐ. Ottawa, Printed by S. E. Dawson, printer to the king's most excellent Majesty, 1897–1904.

1903 contains: Improvement of seeds and seed-grains. The Macdonald funds for manual training and the improvement of rural schools. Progress in dairying.

Cape of Good Hope—*Agriculture, Dept. of.* . . . Reports of the agricultural assistants at Cape Town and Stellenbosch, for the year 1898. 33ᶜᵐ. Cape Town, W. A. Richards & sons, government printers, 1899.

Chavez, Juan Ramón. . . . Investigación agrícola en la provincia de Santiago del Estero . . . 1 p. l., 125 p. 26½ᶜᵐ. Buenos Aires, Compañía Sud-Americana de billetes de banco, 1904. (República Argentina. Anales del Ministerio de agricultura. Sección agricultura; botánica y agronomía. Agronomía, tomo i, n° 8)

Agr 5–320

Colorado—*Agriculture, State board of.* Twenty-sixth annual report of the State board of agriculture and the State agricultural college, including the seventeenth annual report of the agricultural experiment station, Fort Collins, Colo., 1904. 23½ᶜᵐ. Denver, The Smith-Brooks printing co., state printers, 1904.

Crocker, A. An essay on farm buildings, with plans, elevations, &c. Presented to the honourable board of agriculture . . . 7, [1] p. 7 plans. 26½ x 21½ᶜᵐ. [n. p.] 1797.

Agr 5–271

From Communications to the board of agriculture, vol. 1, pt. 1.

Darrow, James Wallace. Origin and early history of the order of Patrons of husbandry in the United States . . . 2 p. l., [9]–55, [1] p. front. (port.) illus. 23ᶜᵐ. Chatham, N. Y. [Courier printing house] 1904.

5–986

Douai, France. Société d'agriculture, des sciences et des arts, centrale du Département du Nord. . . . Bulletin du comice agricole, année 1899, ptie. 2; 1900; 1902, ptie. 1; 1903, ptie. 1; 1904, ptie. 1. 23–24½ᶜᵐ. Douai, Impr. A. Bassée, 1901– [04]

Farmer and stock-breeder year book and country gentleman's almanack for 1905 . . . illus., ports. 24ᶜᵐ. London, The "Farmer and Stock Breeder" [1904]

Gallais, F. Essai de naturalisation des végétaux utiles à l'agriculture entre les parallèles 30°–46° plus particulièrement aux puissances composant le bassin méditerranéen, la province d'Alger prise comme type . . . 108 p. illus. 23½ᶜᵐ. Angoulême, Impr. charentaise de A. Nadaud et cᵉ, 1868.

Agr 5–2

Girola, Carlos D. . . . Investigación agrícola en la República Argentina. Preliminares notas y observaciones sobre los trabajos efectuados hasta febrero de 1904 . . . 406, [2], [407]–414 p. plates, fold. map. 26½ᶜᵐ. Buenos Aires, Compañía Sud-Americana de billetes de banco, 1904. (República Argentina. Anales del Ministerio de agricultura. Sección agricultura; botánica y agronomía. Agronomía, tomo i, no. 1)

Agr 5–315

Graebner, Paul, *i. e.* Carl Otto Robert Peter Paul. Handbuch der heidekultur, unter mitwirkung von Otto von Bentheim . . . und anderer fachmännern . . . viii, 296 p. illus., fold. map. 25½ᶜᵐ. Leipzig, W. Engelman, 1904.

Agr 5–92

Gt. Brit.—*Foreign office.* . . . Reports on the agricultural departments of foreign countries. Presented to the House of commons by command . . . 1 p. l., 59, [1] p. 33ᶜᵐ. London, Printed by Harrison and sons, 1884.

Agr 5–302

At head of title; Commercial, no. 9 (1884)

Guarini, E. L'électricité agricole . . . viii, 162 p. plates. 19½ᶜᵐ. Lausanne, Société suisse d'édition, 1904.

Agr 5–5

Hawaii—*Agriculture and forestry, Commissioner of.* . . . Report of the commissioner of agriculture and forestry for year ending December 31st, 1900; for the biennial period ending December 31st, 1902. 23ᶜᵐ. (1900, 22½ᶜᵐ) Honolulu, Gazette print, 1901–03.

Henderson, Richard. The first principles of agriculture and forestry from an every-day point of view . . . xvi, 408 p. 25ᶜᵐ. London, The Country gentlemen's association, ltd. [1904] (*Half-title:* The Estate library series)

Agr 5–130

Holmberg, Eduardo Alejandro, *jr.* . . . Investigación agrícola en la provincia de Jujuy . . . 177 p. illus., fold. pl., fold. tables. 26½ᶜᵐ. Buenos Aires, Compañía Sud-Americana de billetes de banco, 1904. (República Argentina. Anales del Ministerio de agricultura. Sección agricultura; botánica y agronomia. Agronomía, tomo i, no. 6)

Agr 5–318

Huergo, Ricardo J. . . . Investigación agrícola en la región septentrional de la provincia de Buenos Aires . . . 223 p., 1 l. fold. plans. 26½ᶜᵐ. Buenos Aires, Compañía Sud-Americana de billetes de banco, 1904. (República Argentina. Anales del Ministerio de agricultura. Sección agricultura; botánica y agronomía. Agronomía, tomo I, no. 2) Agr 5—316

India—*Assam—Land records and agriculture, Dept. of.* Report . . . for the fifteen months ending the 30th June 1904. 33ᶜᵐ. Shillong, Printed at the Assam secretariat printing office, 1904.

India—*Bombay presidency—Land records and agriculture, Dept. of.* . . . Report of the Department of agriculture . . . for the year 1903–1904. 32½ᶜᵐ. Bombay, Printed at the Government central press, 1904.

India—*Bombay presidency—Land records and agriculture, Dept. of.* . . . Season and crop report . . . for the year 1903–1904. 33½ᶜᵐ. Bombay, Printed at the Government central press, 1904.

India—*Central Provinces and Berar—Land records and Agriculture, Dept of.* . . . Season and crop report . . . for the year 1903–04. 33½ᶜᵐ. Nagpur, Printed at the Secretariat press, 1904.

India—*Madras presidency—Agriculture, Dept. of.* Report on the operations of the Department of agriculture . . . for the official year 1903–04. 34ᶜᵐ. Madras, Printed by the superintendent, government press, 1904.

India— *Punjab—Land records and agriculture, Dept. of.* . . . Report on the season and crops of the Punjab for the year 1903–1904 . . . tables. 33ᶜᵐ. Lahore, The "Civil and military gazette" press, 1904.

Kansas—*Agriculture, State board of.* Fourteenth biennial report . . . for the years 1903 and 1904 . . . front. (facsim.) illus. 23½ᶜᵐ. Topeka, Kansas dept. of agriculture, 1905.

Kansas state grange, order of patrons of. husbandry. Journal of proceedings . . . 33rd annual meeting Paola, Kansas, December 13, 14, and 15, 1904. 22ᶜᵐ. Olathe, Register print [1904]

Kansas state grange, order of patrons of husbandry. Roster of officers, the Kansas state and subordinate granges 1905–6. 14½ᶜᵐ. [Olathe, Printed by the Olathe register, 1905]

Kentucky—*Agriculture, labor, and statistics, Bureau of.* Fifteenth biennial report . . . 1902–03. col. front., plates (partly fold., partly col.) fold. map. 23ᶜᵐ. Louisville, G. G. Fetter printing co., 1903.

Michigan—*Agriculture, State board of.* Forty-third annual report of the secretary of the State board of agriculture . . . and seventeenth annual report of the experiment station from July 1, 1903, to June 30, 1904. front. (port) illus., plates. 23½ᶜᵐ. Lansing, Wynkoop, Hallenbeck, Crawford co., state printers, 1904.

Michigan state farmers' institutes. Institute bulletin no. 10 . . . 1903–04. 23½ᶜᵐ. Agricultural College, 1904.

Netherlands—*Waterstaat, handel en nijverheid, Departement van—Afdeeling landbouw.* . . . Lijst van vereenigingen op land- en tuinbouwgebied. 85 p., 1 l. 24½ᶜᵐ. 's-Gravenhage, 1905. (Verslagen en mededeelingen van den Afdeeling landbouw van het Departement van waterstaat, handel en nijverheid. 1905, no. 1)

Norway—*Landbrugsdirektør.* Aarsberetning angaaende de offentlige foranstaltninger til landbrugets fremme i aaret 1903. III. Stipendieberetninger . . . illus. 22½ᶜᵐ. Kristiania, Grøndahl & sons bogtrykkeri, 1904.

Nova Scotia—*Agriculture, Secretary for.* Annual report . . . for the year 1904. front., plates, port. 24½ᶜᵐ. Halifax, Commissioner of public works and mines, king's printer, 1905.

Ontario—*Farmers' institutes, Superintendent of.* Annual report . . . 1904. pt. III. Meetings and statistics . . . ports. 24ᶜᵐ. Toronto, Printed by L. K. Cameron, printer to the king's most excellent Majesty, 1905.

Pratt, Edwin A. The organization of agriculture . . . [2d ed.] xii, 443, [1] p. 19½ᶜᵐ. London, J. Murray, 1905.

Queensland—*Agriculture, Dept. of.* . . . Report . . . for the years 1901/02–1902/03. plans. 33½ᶜᵐ. [Brisbane, G. A. Vaughn, government printer, 1902–03]

Raña, Eduardo S. . . . Investigación agrícola en la República Argentina, provincia de Entre Rios . . . v, 326 p. incl. illus., fold. tables. 7 maps (1 fold.) 26½ᶜᵐ. Buenos Aires, Impr. de M. Biedma e hijo, 1904. (República Argentina. Anales del Ministerio de agricultura. Sección agricultura; botánica y agronomía. Agronomía, tomo I, núm. 4)   Agr 5—324

La Revista agrícola. Periódico quincenal destinado exclusivamente á la propagación de los conocimientos y adelantos agrícolas y á la defensa de los intereses de la agricultura mexicana . . . tomo XIX. illus. 32½ᶜᵐ. México, Oficina tipográfica de la Secretaría de fomento, 1904.

Royal agricultural society of England. Journal . . . v. 65. front. (port.) illus., plates, fold. plans. 22½ᶜᵐ. London, J. Murray, 1904.

Semler, Heinrich. Die tropische agrikultur. Ein handbuch für pflanzer und kaufleute . . . 2. aufl. Unter mitwirkung von generalsekretär M. Busemann und professor Dr. O. Warburg bearb. und hrsg. von Dr. Richard Hindorf. 3. bd. illus. 24½ᶜᵐ. Wismar, Hinstorff'sche hofbuchhandlung verlagskonto, 1903.

The **Southern** agriculturist and register of rural affairs; adapted to the southern section of the United States. Vol. I, for the year 1828 . . . 21½ᶜᵐ. Charleston, A. E. Miller, 1828.

Strakosch, Siegfried. Amerikanische landwirtschaft. Eine reisestudie . . . 3 p. l., 187 p. illus., fold. map. 25½ᶜᵐ. Wien, W. Frick, 1905.   Agr 5—294

Tasmania—*Agriculture, Council of.* Report for 1899, 1901. 34–34½ᶜᵐ. [Hobart, J. Vail, government printer, 1900–1902]

—— Interim report for 1903. 33½ᶜᵐ. [Hobart, J. Vail, government printer, 1903]

Tidsskrift for landbrugets planteavl. Hovedorgan for statens forsøg og undersøgelser vedrørende markens avlsplanter. Redigeret af E. Rostrup. 1.–4. bind. 23½ᶜᵐ. Kjøbenhavn, T. Linds efterfølger Eckardt & Trandsen, 1895–98.

Utah—*Farmers' institutes.* . . . Annual no. 7 . . . for the fiscal year ending October 31, 1904. illus. (incl. front.) plates. 21ᶜᵐ. Provo, The Skelton pub. co. [1904]

The **Western** farmers' almanac 1905. Containing original forecasts of the weather for the entire year; with original articles for the practical farmer by well-known authors. illus. 23ᶜᵐ. Louisville, Ky., J. P. Morton & co. [1904]

Wisconsin farmers' institutes. . . . A handbook of agriculture. Bulletin no. 18, 1904 . . . front., illus. (incl. ports.) 22ᶜᵐ. Madison, Democrat printing co., printer [1904]

Yssouribehere, Pedro J. . . . Investigación agrícola en el territorio de Misiones . . . 222 p. incl. plates. fold. maps. 26½ᶜᵐ. Buenos Aires, Compañía Sud-Americana de billetes de banco, 1904. (República Argentina. Anales del Ministerio de agricultura. Sección agricultura; botánica y agronomía. Agronomía, tomo I, no. 9)   Agr 5—321

2. AGRICULTURAL EDUCATION.

Alabama—*Polytechnic institute, Auburn.* Catalogue . . . 1903. front., plates (1 fold.) fold. plan. 23^{cm}. Montgomery, The Brown printing company, printers and binders, 1903.

Chile—*Instituto agrícola—Asociación de antiguos alumnos.* Anuario . . . año III, 1904. illus., ports., plates (1 fold.) 26$\frac{1}{2}^{cm}$. Santiago de Chile, Imprenta del Instituto agrícola, 1904.

Clemson agricultural college of South Carolina. Fifteenth annual report of the board of trustees . . . 1904. 23^{cm}. Columbia, The State company, printers, 1905.

Colorado—*State agricultural college.* Twenty-fourth annual register of the officers and students . . . 1902/03. plan. 19^{cm}. Fort Collins, Courier print [1903]

Delaware—*College, Newark.* Catalogue of the officers and students . . . for the year 1902/03. 23^{cm}. [Wilmington, The J. M. Rogers press, 1903]

Gloucestershire, *Eng.—Education committee* . . . Report of the conference on agricultural education held at Gloucester on October 15th, 1904. Ed. by Charles Bathurst, jr., M. A., and John C. Medd, M. A. 1 p. l., ii, 220 p. 21$\frac{1}{2}^{cm}$. Gloucester, Chance & Bland, 1904. Agr 5—298

Gt. Brit.—*Agriculture and fisheries, board of.* . . . Annual report on the distribution of grants for agricultural education and research in the year 1903/04 . . . 24$\frac{1}{2}^{cm}$. London, Printed for H. M. Stationery off., by Darling & Son, ltd., 1904.

Iowa—*State college of agriculture and the mechanic arts.* . . . Catalog, 1902/03. 19^{cm}. Ames, By the college, 1903.

Kentucky—*State college, Lexington.* Catalogue of the officers, studies, and students . . . for the session ending June 4, 1903. 22^{cm}. Lexington, Press of J. M. Byrnes, 1903.

Michigan—*Agricultural college.* Officers and students . . . for the year 1902/03, together with other general information concerning the college. 46th year. illus. 23^{cm}. Agricultural college, Published by the college, 1903.

New Mexico—*College of agriculture and mechanic arts.* . . . Morrill reports for 1901–02. no. 12. 22$\frac{1}{2}^{cm}$. [n. p., 1902]

Oklahoma—*Agricultural and mechanical college.* . . . Annual catalogue, 1903–4, with announcements for 1904–5. plates. 23$\frac{1}{2}^{cm}$. Stillwater [College press, 1904]

Princess Anne academy, eastern branch, Maryland agricultural college. [Catalogue 1903/04] illus. 23^{cm}. Baltimore, Thomas & Evans, printers [1903]

Rhode Island—*College of agriculture and mechanic arts, Kingston.* Sixteenth annual report. pt. III. Catalogue . . . fold. front., plates. 23^{cm}. Providence, E. L. Freeman & sons, printers to the state, 1904.

Southern university and agricultural and mechanical college, *New Orleans, La.* Catalogue . . . 1902/03. fronts, plates. 23^{cm}. [New Orleans] Southern university and A. & M. college printing office, 1903.

Tabor, *Bohemia.* **Königliche böhmische landwirthschaftliche akademie.** Čtvrtá výroční zpráva o Král. české hospodářské akademii v Táboře za školní rok 1903–04 . . . 25$\frac{1}{2}^{cm}$. Táboře [Tiskem P. Franka] 1904.

Texas—*Agricultural and mechanical college.* 27th–28th annual catalogue, session 1902/03–1903/04 . . . 23^{cm}. Austin, Von Boeckmann-Jones, state printers, 1903–04.

Virginia—*Agricultural and mechanical college and polytechnic institute, Blacksburg, Va.* Catalogue . . . 1902/03. 23^{cm}. Lynchburg, J. P. Bell company, printers, 1903.

Weilburg (*Prussia*) **Landwirtschaftsschule.** Siebenundzwanzigstes programm . . . mit welchem über das schuljahr 1903/04 berichtet der direktor . . . 26½ x 22ᶜᵐ. Weilburg, Druck von H. Zipper, 1904.

3. EXPERIMENT STATIONS.

Arizona—*Agricultural experiment station.* . . . Fifteenth annual report. For the year ending June 30, 1904 . . . illus. 22½ᶜᵐ. Tucson, 1904.

Breslau, Universität—*Landwirtschaftliches institut.* Mitteilungen . . . 2. bd., hft. v; 3. bd., hft. ɪ. illus., plates, fold. tables. 25½ᶜᵐ. Berlin, P. Parey, 1904.

British Guiana—*Agriculture, Board of.* . . . Report on the agricultural work in the experimental fields and the Government laboratory, for the year 1903–04. 33ᶜᵐ. Georgetown, Demerara, Est. of J. C. Jardine, decd., printers to the government, 1904.

California—*University*—*Agricultural experiment station.* . . . Report of work . . . from June 30, 1903, to June 30, 1904. Being a part of the report of the regents of the university. illus., fold. tab. 22½ᶜᵐ. Sacramento, W. W. Shannon, superintendent state printing, 1904.
At head of title: University of California publications.

Connecticut—*Agricultural experiment station.* . . . Report . . . for the year ending October 31, 1904. pt. ɪɪ. Food products. illus., pl. 23ᶜᵐ. [New Haven, 1904]

Cornell university—*Agricultural experiment station.* Seventeenth annual report . . . 1904. illus., plates. 22½ᶜᵐ. Ithaca, The University, 1904.

Durham college of science, *Newcastle-upon-Tyne*—*Agricultural dept.* . . . Twelfth annual report on field and other experiments, 1903 . . . 21½ᶜᵐ. London and Newcastle-upon-Tyne, A. Reid and company, limited, 1904.
At head of title: County councils of Cumberland, Durham and Northumberland.

Goes (*Netherlands*) **Rijkslandbouwproefstation.** Verslag . . . over 1903 . . . 24ᶜᵐ. 's Gravenhage, Gebrs. J. & H. von Langenhuysen, 1904.
Overgedrukt uit de ,,Verslagen en mededeelingen van de Afdeeling landbouw van het Departement van waterstaat, handel en nijverheid.'' 1904. no. 6.

Halle Universität—*Landwirtschaftliches institut.* Berichte aus dem physiologischen laboratorium und der versuchsanstalt . . . hrsg. von Dr. Julius Kuhn. 17. hft. illus., fold. tab. 28½ᶜᵐ. Leipzig, R. C. Schmidt & co., 1904.

Harper-Adams agricultural college, *Newport, Shropshire, England.* Field experiments in Staffordshire and Shropshire and at the Harper-Adams agricultural college, Newport, Salop. Joint report for season 1904. 23ᶜᵐ. Newport, B. Horne, Smallman & co. (limited), printers, etc., [1905]

Illinois—*University*—*Agricultural experiment station.* Seventeenth annual report · . . for the year ending June 30, 1904. 23ᶜᵐ. Urbana, 1904.

India—*Bombay presidency*—*Agriculture, Deputy director of.* Annual report on the experimental farms . . . for the year ending 31st March, 1904. 33ᶜᵐ. Bombay, Printed at the Government central press, 1904.

India—*Central provinces*—*Government.* Report on the management of the district gardens . . . for the year 1903–04. 33½ᶜᵐ. Nagpur, Printed at the Secretariat press, 1904.

India—*United Provinces of Agra and Oudh*—*Land records and agriculture, Dept. of.* Report on the Cawnpore farm and other experiment stations in the United Provinces for the year ending June 30th, 1904. 33½ᶜᵐ. Allahabad, Printed at the United Provinces government press, 1904.

Koulikoro, *Haut-Sénégal et Niger, Africa.* **Station agronomique.** [Report 1902–04] 22½ᶜᵐ. [Koulikoro, 1904]
Manuscript.

Leipzig, Universität—*Landwirtschäftliches institut.* Mitteilungen . . . Hrsg. von Dr. W. Kirchner . . . 5. hft. viii diagr. 25^{cm}. Berlin, P. Parey, 1904.

Malta—*Experimental farm station.* Report 1903/04. 32^{cm}. [C. Balzan?, 1904]

Nebraska—*Agricultural experiment station.* . . . Eighteenth annual report . . . pt. 1. 23^{cm}. Lincoln, 1905.

Netherlands—*Waterstaat, handel en nijverheid, Departement—Afdeeling landbouw.* . . . Verslagen der rijkslandbouwproefstations over 1903. 137 p. 24^{cm}. s'-Gravenhage, 1904. (Verslagen en mededeelingen van de Afdeeling landbouw van het Departement van waterstaat, handel en nijverheid. 1904, no. 6)

Norges landbrugshøiskole. Aarsberetning om . . . akervekstforsøg i 1902 og 1903 af Bastian R. Larsen . . . illus., col. pl. 22½^{cm}. Kristiania, Johansen & Nielsens bogtrykkeri, 1905.

Northumberland county—*Education committee.* . . . . Eighth annual report on experiments with crops and stock at the county demonstration farm, Cockle Park, Morpeth . . . 1903/04. fold. tab. 21½^{cm}. Newcastle-on-Tyne, R. Ward & sons, printers, 1905.

Ploti, Sel'sko-khoziaïstvennaia opuitnaia stantziia. Godichnuiĭ otchet Plotianskoĭ sel'sko-khoziaïstvennoĭ opuitnoĭ stantzii kniazia P. P. Trubetzkago . . . Neuvième rapport annuel pour l'année 1903 de la station expérimentale agronomique à Ploty . . . fondée par le prince Paul Troubetzkoy. fold. plates, fold. tables. 27^{cm}. Odessa, 1904.

Rheinischer bauern-verein in Kempen. *Landwirtschaftliche versuchsstation.* Bericht über die tätigkeit . . . in den jahren 1902 und 1903 . . . 21½^{cm}. [n. p., n. d.]

Russia—*Zemledieliia i gosudarstvennykh imushchestv, Ministerstvo—Zemledieliia, Departament [Agriculture and crown lands, Ministry of—Agriculture, Dept. of]* . . . Ezhegodnik Russkikh sel'skokhoziaïstvennykh opytnykh uchrezhdeniĭ. no. 1. 27^{cm}. S_t-Peterburg, Tipografiia V. Kirshbauma, 1901. Year-book of Russian agricultural experimental institutions.

Le Stazioni sperimentali agrarie italiane . . . 1872–92. v. i–xxiii. illus. plates. 25–26½^{cm}. Asti, tipografia operaia A. Bianchi, 1872–93. No. 2 of v. 19 wanting.

Storrs agricultural experiment station. . . . Sixteenth annual report . . . for the year ending June 30, 1904. illus. 23½^{cm}. Middletown, Conn., Pelton & King, printers and bookbinders, 1904.

Wisconsin—*University—Agricultural experiment station.* Twenty-first annual report . . . for the year ending June 30, 1904. front., illus., plates. 22½^{cm}. Madison, Democrat printing co., state printer, 1904.

4. SEEDS.

California—*University—Agricultural experiment station.* Exchange seed-list, March, 1898; 1898–99. 23½–24^{cm}. Berkeley, The University press, 1898–1900.

Cambridge (*Eng.*) **Botanic garden.** Delectus seminum ex Horto cantabrigiensis academiæ ad mutuam commutationem propositorum Jan°, 1905. 21½^{cm}. Cantabrigiæ, Typis academicis, 1905.

Canadian seed growers' association. Minutes of first annual meeting at Ottawa, June 15th and 16th, 1904. Constitution, by-laws, and regulations with general explanations of the regulations regarding the growing, selecting, and preserving of seeds intended for registration. 25^{cm}. Ottawa, Government printing bureau, 1904.

Dansk frøkontrol. Aarsberetning . . . 33. arbejdsaar 1903–04, af K. Dorph-Petersen. '22½ᶜᵐ. København, Trykt hos J. Jørgensen & co. (M. A. Hannover) 1904.

Göteborgs och Bohus läns frökontrollanstalt. Redogörelse för . . . verksamhet under arbetsåret i juli, 1902 till 30 juni 1903, juli 1903 till juni 1904. 20ᶜᵐ. [Göteborg, W. Zachrissons boktryckeri A.–B., 1904–05]

Hernösand, Frokontrollanstalt i. Berättelse öfver verksamheten . . . under arbetsåret 1/7 1901–30/6 1902, 1/7 1902–30/6 1903. 20ᶜᵐ. Hernosänd, Hernösands-postens tryckeri-aktiebolag, 1903–04.

Luleå, Sweden. **Kemisk-växtbiologiska anstalt och frökontrollanstalt.** Berättelse öfver verksamketen . . . år 1903. 23ᶜᵐ. [Luleå, Hallman & Helens boktryckeriaktiebolag, 1904]
Separattryck af Norrbattens läns hushållningssällskaps handlingar 1903–04.

Lund, *Sweden.* **Frökontrollanstalt.** Verksamhet år 1903. 20½ᶜᵐ. Malmö, Förlags-aktiebolagets boktryckeri, 1904.

Lyon, Thomas Lyttleton. Examining and grading grains, by T. L. Lyon . . . and E. G. Montgomery . . . 64 p: illus. 22ᶜᵐ. [Lincoln?] Published by the authors, 1904.   Agr 5—563

Molkom, *Sweden.* **Vermlands läns frökontrollanstalt, kemiska laboratorium och mjölkkontrollanstalt.** Redogörelse för analysarbetena . . . år 1903 jemte kort öfversikt af anstalternas 10-åriga verksamhet . . . 20ᶜᵐ. Karlstad, Nya Wermlands-tidningens aktiebolag, 1904.

Portici, *Italy.* **Regia scuola superiore d'agricoltura in—**Orto, botanico. . . . Catalogo dei semi raccolti nell' anno 1904. 24ᶜᵐ. [Portici, 1904]

Rodewald, Hermann. Untersuchungen über die fehler der samenprüfungen. Auf veranlassung der Deutschen landwirtschafts-gesellschaft ausgeführt von zahlreichen samenprüfungs-anstalten des Deutschen reiches. 1 p. l., iv p., 1 l., 117 p. 24ᶜᵐ. Berlin, Deutsche landwirtschafts-gesellschaft, 1904. (*Added t.-p.:* Arbeiten der Deutschen landwirtschafts-gesellschaft . . . hft. 101.)   Agr 5—134

Stockholms läns hushållningssällskaps frökontrollanstalt. Redogörelse för verksamheten under arbetsåret den 1/7 1903—30/6 1904 af anstaltens förestandare. 23ᶜᵐ. Stockholm, Centraltryckeriet, 1905.

Switzerland—Samenuntersuchungs- und versuchs-anstalt in Zürich. Siebenundzwanzigster jahresbericht . . . illus. 24½ᶜᵐ. Zürich, 1905.
Separat-abdruck aus dem Landwirtschaftlichen jahrbuch der Schweiz.

Vienna. **Universität—**Botanischer garten. . . . Verzeichnis von sämereien, welche 1904 gesammelt wurden und zum tausche angeboten werden . . . 22½ᶜᵐ. [Wien, Druck von K. Groák, 1905]

Villa Thuret, *Antibes, France—*Laboratoire pour les études de culture et de botanique. Catalogue des graines récoltées en 1904. 25ᶜᵐ. [Antibes, 1905]

Wageningen. **Rijksproefstation voor zaadecontrole.** Catalogue des graines récoltées en 1904. 21ᶜᵐ. [n. p., 1904]

5. SOILS AND FERTILIZERS.

Baker, Moses Nelson. British sewage works and notes on the sewage farms of Paris and on two German works . . . 146, [3] p. 24ᶜᵐ. New York, The Engineering news publishing co., 1904.   4—27877

Barré, O. L'architecture du sol de la France; essai de géographie tectonique . . . 2 p. l., iii, 393 p., 1 l. incl. plans. fold. plans. 25ᶜᵐ. Paris, A. Colin, 1903. Agr 5—269

Great Britain—*Agriculture and fisheries, Board of—Departmental committee appointed to inquire into and report upon the working in Great Britain of the fertilisers & feeding stuffs* *act, 1898.* Report . . . with copy of minutes appointing the committee. Presented to both Houses of Parliament by command of His Majesty. iii, 38 p. 33½ᶜᵐ. London, Printed for H. M. Stationery off. by Wyman & sons, limited, 1905.

Hungary—*Königl. ungar. ackerbauminister.* . . . A világ 1904 évi gabonatermese . . . 31ᶜᵐ. Budapest, Pallas részvénytársaság nyomdája, 1904.

Lawes, *Sir* John Bennet, *1st bart.* Agricultural chemistry. On the growth of barley by different manures, continuously on the same land; and on the position of the crop in rotation. By J. B. Lawes and Dr. J. H. Gilbert . . . From the Journal of the Royal agricultural society of England, vol. xviii, pt. ii; with supplementary results in tables xvi–xviii; and some alterations of the succeeding text accordingly. 80 p. illus. 21ᶜ¹. London, Printed by W. Clowes & sons, 1858. Agr 5—598

Lawes, Sir John Bennet, *1st bart.* Report of experiments on the growth of wheat for twenty years in succession on the same land. By J. B. Lawes . . . & J. H. Gilbert . . . iv, [5]–109, xli p. fold. tab. 21ᶜᵐ. London, Printed by W. Clowes and sons, 1864. [*With his* Agricultural chemistry. On the growth of barley. London, 1858] Agr 5—597
"From the Journal of the Royal agricultural society of England, vol. xxv, pts. I & II."

Lawes, Sir John Bennet, *1st bart.* Report of experiments with different manures on permanent meadow land. By J. B. Lawes . . . & Dr. J. H. Gilbert . . . 2 p. l., 111, [1] p. 21ᶜᵐ. London, Printed by W. Clowes and sons, 1859. [*With his* Agricultural chemistry. On the growth of barley. London, 1858] Agr 5—599
"From the Journal of the Royal agricultural society of England, vol. XIX–XX."

Ohio—*Agriculture, State board of.* Official report . . . on commercial fertilizers licensed to be sold during the year 1904. 23½ᶜᵐ. Springfield, The Springfield publishing company, state printers [1905]

Orth, Albert. Kalk- und mergel-düngung. Anleitung für den praktischen landwirt . . . x, 224 p. 18ᶜᵐ. Berlin, Druck von Gebr. Unger, 1896. (*Added t.-p.:* Anleitungen für den praktischen landwirt. Hrsg. vom direktorium der Deutschen landwirtschafts-gesellschaft. Der sammlung nr. 5) Agr 5—267

Svenska mosskulturförening. Gödslingsförsok utförda af Svenska mosskultur-föreningen åren 1887–1899 under ledning af direktör Carl von Feilitzen. 2 p. l., 282 p. front. (port.) illus., col. tables. 32ᶜᵐ. Göteborg, W. Zachrissons boktryckeri, 1901. (*On cover:* Bilage till Svenska mosskulturföreningens tidskrift n:o 4 för 1901) Agr 5—296

Voelcker, John Christopher Augustus. Absorption of potash by soils of known composition . . . 22 p. 21½ᶜᵐ. London, Printed by W. Clowes and sons, 1864. [*With his* On milk. London, 1863]
."From the Journal of the Royal agricultural society of England, vol. xxv, pt. II."

Voelcker, John Christopher Augustus. . . . Annual report. 10 p. 21½ᶜᵐ. London, Printed by W. Clowes and sons, 1866. [*With his* On milk. London, 1863]
"From the Journal of the Royal agricultural society of England, vol. II—S. S., pt. I."

Voelcker, John Christopher Augustus. Annual report of chemical analyses, etc. . . . 10 p. 21½ᶜᵐ. London, Printed by W. Clowes and sons, 1865. [*With his* On milk. London, 1863]
"From the Journal of the Royal agricultural society of England, S. S.—vol. I, pt. I."

Voelcker, John Christopher Augustus. Annual report on adulterations, etc. . . . 8 p. 21½ᶜⁿ. London, Printed by W. Clowes and sons, 1864. [*With his* On milk. London, 1863]
"From the Journal of the Royal agricultural society of England, vol. xxv, pt. I."

Voelcker, John Christopher Augustus. Experiments with different top-dressings upon wheat. 18 p. 21½ᶜᵐ. London, Printed by W. Clowes and sons, 1862. [*With his* On milk. London, 1863]
"From the Journal of the Royal agricultural society of England, vol. XXIII."

Voelcker, John Christopher Augustus. Field experiments of crude German potash-salts and common salt on mangolds . . . 8 p. 21½^{cm}. London, Printed by W. Clowes and sons, 1867. [*With his* On milk. London, 1863]
"From the Journal of the Royal agricultural society of England, vol. III.—S. S., pt. I."

Voelcker, John Christopher Augustus. Field experiments on clover-seeds . . . 21 p. 21½^{cm}. London, Printed by W. Clowes and sons, 1866. [*With his* On milk. London, 1863]
"From the Journal of the Royal agricultural society of England, vol. II.—S. S., pt. II."

Voelcker, John Christopher Augustus. Field experiments on root-crops . . . 23 p. 21½^{cm}. London, Printed by W. Clowes and sons, 1867. [*With his* On milk. London, 1863]
"From the Journal of the Royal agricultural society of England, vol. III—S. S., pt. II."

Voelcker, John Christopher Augustus. On some causes of unproductiveness in soils . . . 20 p. . 21½^{cm}. London, Printed by W. Clowes and sons, 1865. [*With his* On milk. London, 1863]
"From the Journal of the Royal agricultural society of England, S. S.—vol. I, pt. I."

Voelcker, John Christopher Augustus. On the composition and nutritive value of Anthyllis vulneraria (lady's fingers) as a fodder plant. 6 p. 21½^{cm}. London, Printed by W. Clowes and sons, 1867. [*With his* On milk. London, 1863]
"From the Journal of the Royal agricultural society of England, vol. III—S. S., pt. II."

Voelcker, John Christopher Augustus. On the composition and value of Norwegian apatite, Spanish phosphorite, coprolites, and other phosphatic materials used in England for agricultural purposes . . . 34 p. 21^{cm}. London, Printed by W. Clowes and sons, 1861. [*With* Lawes, Sir John B. Agricultural chemistry. On the growth of barley. London, 1858]   Agr 5—595
"From the Journal of the Royal agricultural society of England, vol. XXI, pt. II."

Voelcker, John Christopher Augustus. On the functions of soda-salts in agriculture . . . 21 p. 21½^{cm}. London, Printed by W. Clowes and sons, 1865. [*With his* On milk. London, 1863]
"From the Journal of the Royal agricultural society of England, vol. I—S. S., pt. II."

Voelcker, John Christopher Augustus. Peruvian guano and the means of increasing its efficacy as a manure . . . 26 p. 21½^{cm}. London, Printed by W. Clowes and sons, 1864. [*With his* On milk. London, 1863]
"From the Journal of the Royal agricultural society of England, vol. xxv, pt. I."

Voelcker, John Christopher Augustus. Report of the improvement of grass-land on Mr. E. Ruck's manor farm, Braydon, Wilts. By Dr. A. Voelcker and Professor Coleman. 19 p. 21½^{cm}. London, Printed by W. Clowes and sons, 1866. [*With his* On milk. London, 1863]
"From the Journal of the Royal agricultural society of England, vol. II—S. S., pt. II."

Voelcker, John Christopher Augustus. . . . Report on field experiments and laboratory researches on the constituents of manures essential to cultivated crops . . . [1], [158]–173 p. 21½^{cm}. London, Printed by Taylor and Francis, 1862. [*With his* On milk. London, 1863]
From the Report of the British association for the advancement of science for 1861.

Voelcker, John Christopher Augustus. Salt experiments and mangolds . . . 6 p. 21½^{cm}. London, Printed by W. Clowes and sons, 1864. [*With his* On milk. London, 1863]
"From the Journal of the Royal agricultural society of England, vol. xxv, pt. I."

Wohltmann, Ferdinand. . . . Die wirkung der kochsalzdüngung auf unsere feldfrüchte. 20 p. 22^{cm}. Bonn, C. Georgi, 1904. (. . . VII. bericht des Instituts für bodenlehre und pflanzenbau der Landwirtschaftlichen akademie Bonn-Poppelsdorf . . .)
Sonderabdruck aus der Landwirtschaftlichen zeitschrift für die Rheinprovinz, 5. jahrg., 1904, nr. 46 und 47.

6. IRRIGATION.

Colorado—*Legislature.* Water rights in Colorado and irrigation laws of 1899, 1901, 1903, measurement division and duty of water, by E. L. Rogers . . . 24 p. 15x7½^{cm}. Denver, Colo., W. F. Robinson printing co. [1904?]

Müller, Richard. Die entwässerungs-genossenschaft, ihre gründung, leitung und buchführung . . . 1 p. l., 119, il, [2] p. 24½^{cm}. Prag, Verlag der Deutschen section des Landesculturrathes für das königreich Böhmen, 1900. (*Added t-p.:* Arbeiten der Deutschen section des Landesculturrathes für das königreich Böhmen . . . hft. III) Agr 5—123

Cover and added t.-p. give date as 1901.

Spain—*Junta consultiva agronómica.* . . . El regadío en España. Resumen hecho por la Junta consultiva agronómica de las memorias sobre riegos remitidas por los ingenieros del Servicio agronómico provincial. 277, [2] p., 2 l. 24^{cm}. Madrid, Imprenta de los hijos de M. G. Hernández, 1904. Agr 5—132

At head of title: Ministerio de agricultura, industria, comercio y obras públicas. Dirección general de agricultura.

Washington (*state*)—*Arid lands, Commissioner of.* . . . Second biennial report . . . Arid lands and irrigation in Washington . . . 23^{cm}. Olympia, G. Hicks, state printer, 1898.

—— Supplemental report . . . cover-title, 10 p. 22½^{cm}. [Olympia, 1898]

7. PLANT DISEASES.

Ascárate y Fernández, Casildo. Insectos y criptógamas que invaden los cultivos en España . . . 780 p. illus., VIII col. pl. 25½^{cm}. Madrid, Tipolitografía de L. Peánt e hijos, 1893. Agr 5—57

Guéguen, Fernand. Les maladies parasitaires de la vigne (parasites végétaux et parasites animaux) . . . Préface de M. Maxime Radais . . . 2 p. l., vi, 198 p. illus. 18^{cm}. Paris, O. Doin [etc.] 1904. (*Half-title:* Bibliothèque d'horticulture (encyclopédie horticole) publiée sous la direction de M. le Dr F. Heim) Agr 5—33

Klitzing, Heinrich. Der apfelbaum, seine feinde und krankheiten . . . chart of 102x77^{cm}. Frankfurt a. Oder, Trowitzsch & sohn [190–]

Mann, Harold H. . . . Red rust; a serious blight of the tea plant (2d ed.) by Harold H. Mann . . . and C. M. Hutchinson . . . 2 p. l., 26 p. VII pl. (3 col.) 25^{cm}. Calcutta, Printed at the city press, 1904. (Indian tea association [Publication] 1904, no. 4) Agr 5—305

Each col. pl. accompanied by guard sheet with description.

Nypels, Paul. . . . Maladies de plantes cultivées. I. Maladie vermiculaire des phlox . . . II. Maladie du houblon . . . 2 p. l., 30 p., 1 l. II pl. 23^{cm}. Bruxelles, A. Castaigne, 1899. Agr 5—285

Extrait des Annales de la Société belge de microscopie. t. XXIII, p. 7 à 39.

Rose, Otto. Der flugbrand der sommergetreidesaaten und massnahmen zur bekämpfung dieses pilzes in der landwirtschaftlichen praxis . . . 59 p., 1 l. 2 pl., fold. tables. 22½^{cm}. Rostock, F. G. Tiedemann nachfl., 1903. Agr 5—118

Inaug.-dis.—Rostock.

8. FIELD CROPS AND INDUSTRIAL PLANTS.

Breda de Haan, J. van. . . . De huidige stand der rijstcultuur in Noord-Italië. 1 p. l., II p., 1 l., 74 p. 26^{cm}. Batavia, G. Kolff & co., 1904. (Mededeelingen uit 's Lands plantentuin LXXIV) Agr 5—297

[**Bugbee,** James M.] Cocoa and chocolate; a short history of their production and use: Rev. ed. . . . 69 p. incl. front., illus. 24½^{cm}. Dorchester, Mass., W. Baker & co., limited, 1904.

        5—2470

Buitenzorg, *Java.* **Jardin botanique.** Mededeelingen uit 's Lands planten-tuin LXXIII. Onderzoekingen aan het proefstation voor indigo in de jaren 1903 en 1904, door J. Hazewinkel . . . Mej. G. Wilbrink . . . diagrs. 26^{cm}. Batavia, G. Kolff & co., 1904.

Chapman, Sydney John. The Lancashire cotton industry; a study in economic development. 2 p. l., VII p., 1 l., 309, [1] p. 23½^{cm}. Manchester, The University press, 1904. (*Half-title:* Publications of the University of Manchester. Economic series. No. 1)

        5—4507

"Bibliography": p. 277-304.

Chijs, J. A. van der. Geschiedenis van de gouvernements thee-cultuur op Java, zamengesteld voornamelijk uit officiëele bronnen . . . Uitgegeven met medewerking van de N.-I. Regeering door de N.-I. Maatschappij van nijverheid en landbouw. viii, 604 p. 27^{cm}. Batavia, Landsdrukkerij; 's Hage, M. Nijhoff, 1903.

        Agr 5—127

Girola, Carlos D. . . . Concursos agrícolas. I. Concurso entre los cultivadores de trigo de la República Argentina. II. Concurso entre los cultivadores de maíz de la República Argentina . . . 70 p., 1 l. plates, fold. tables. 26½^{cm}. Buenos Aires, Compañia Sud-Americana de billetes de banco, 1904. (República Argentina. Anales del Ministerio de agricultura. Sección agricultura; botánica y agronomía. Agronomía. tomo II. no. 1)

        Agr 5—322

Graas, Robert. Der hopfenbau Böhmens. Eine übersichtliche darstellung der hopfenkultur und der hopfenbau-verhältnisse in Böhmen . . . 102 p. illus., fold. plates, double map. 26^{cm}. Prag. Verlag der Deutschen sektion des Landeskultur-rates für das königreich Böhmen, 1904. (*On cover:* Arbeiten der Deutschen sektion des Landeskulturrates für das königreich Böhmen. hft. VII)

        Agr 5—122

Hailer, H. Deutschlands kartoffel-absatz. Statistische untersuchungen über den in- und ausländischen kartoffelbau und kartoffelhandel . . . 4 p. l., 136 p. col. plates (partly fold.) fold. map. 24½^{cm}. Berlin, Deutsche landwirtschafts-gesell-schaft, 1904. (*Added t.-p.:* Arbeiten der Deutschen landwirtschafts-gesellschaft . . . hft. 93)

        Agr 5—258

"Quellen-angaben": p. [131]-132.

Hawaiian sugar planters' association—*Experiment station committee.* Report . . . for the year ending September 30, 1904. plates. 23^{cm}. [Honolulu, 1904.]

Hunt, Thomas Forsyth. The cereals in America . . . XXVII, 421 p. incl. front., illus., diagrs. 20^{cm}. New York, O. Judd company; London, K. Paul, French [!] Trubner & co., limited, 1904.

        4–37016

"Collateral reading" at end of some of the chapters.

Juhlin-Dannfelt, Hermann Julius. . . . Undersökningar af i Sverige odlade rotfrukter. Meddelande i Kungl. Landtbruks-akademien af H. Juhlin Dannfelt och H. G. Söderbaum. 56 p. 24^{cm}. Stockholm, P. A. Norstedt & söner, 1904. (Meddelanden från Kungl. Landtbruks-akademiens experimentalfält. n:o 80)

        Agr 5—314

Louisiana sugar planters' association. [Proceedings of] regular monthly meeting, May 14, 1885. 23^{cm}. [n. p., n. d.]

New South Wales—*Agriculture, Dept. of.* Miscellaneous publication, no. 104. The absorption of water by the gluten of different wheats, by F. B. Guthrie. 24½^{cm}. Sydney, C. Potter, government printer, 1896.

Another of this series bears the title: "Note on imported wheat and flour," and is also no. 104.

Radisson. . . . La badiane; culture—distillation—commerce . . . 8 p. 27^{cm}. Paris, Revue des colonies et des pays de protectorat, 1898. (Petite collection militaire & coloniale L. Brunet. Les cultures coloniales)

Southern Rhodesia—*Agriculture, Dept. of.* . . . Fibre investigations: bulletin no. 1. Cotton by E. R. Sawer . . . 24½ᶜᵐ. Salisbury, Argus printing & publishing company, limited, 1904.

Voelcker, John Christopher Augustus. On the composition of orange globe mangolds, bulbs, and tops . . . 10 p. 21½ᶜᵐ. London, 1866. [*With his* On milk. London, 1863.]
"From the Journal of the Royal agricultural society of England, vol. I—S. S., pt. II."

West Indies (*British*)—*Agriculture, Imperial Dept. of.* Pamphlet series, no. 32 . . . Summary of the results on the cultivation of seedling and other canes at the experiment stations at Barbados, 1904. 18½ᶜᵐ. [Barbados] Commissioner of agriculture, 1904.

Wohltmann, Ferdinand. . . . Ein beitrag zur futterrübenzüchtung insbesondere der Oberndorfer. 19, [1] p. 23½ᶜᵐ. Berlin, "Die Deutsche zuckerindustrie," 1905. (. . . x. bericht des Institutes für bodenlehre und pflanzenbau der Landwirtschaftlichen akademie Bonn-Poppelsdorf)
Sonderabdruck aus "Blätter für zuckerrübenbau," XII. jahrg, (1905), nr. 1 u. flgde.

Wohltmann, Ferdinand. . . . Erträge und haltbarkeit der verbreitetsten deutschen, französischen und englischen futterrüben-sorten . . . cover-title, 30 p. incl. tables. 28½ᶜᵐ. Berlin, Verlag der "Deutschen tageszeitung, druckerei und verlag aktien-gesellschaft," 1905. (Bericht VIII des Instituts für bodenlehre und pflanzenbau der Landw. akademie Bonn-Poppelsdorf)
Sonder-abdruck aus Illustrierte landwirtschaftliche zeitung.

Wye, *Kent.* **South-eastern agricultural college.** . . . Hop experiments, 1903–1904. illus., VIII pl., diagrs. 21ᶜᵐ. [London, Headley brothers, printers, 1904]
1903, reprinted from the South-eastern agricultural college journal, no. 18, June, 1904.
1904 is Bulletin 1, 1904–5.

9. HORTICULTURE AND LANDSCAPE GARDENING.

Alexandria (*Egypt*) horticultural society. . . . Report—accounts and list of members 1904. 23ᶜᵐ. Alexandria, J. C. Lagoudakis, printer [1905]

American cranberry growers' association. Proceedings of the 35th annual meeting . . . January 25, 1905. 22ᶜᵐ. [n. p.] 1905.

Batson, *Mrs.* Henrietta M. A concise handbook of garden flowers . . . vii, 256 p. 17½ᶜᵐ. London, Methuen & co., 1903.   Agr 5—107

Brace, Josh. The culture of fruit trees in pots . . . xi, 110 p. front., illus., plates. 20ᶜᵐ. London, J. Murray, 1904.   Agr 5—264

Curtis, Charles H. The book of topiary, by Charles H. Curtis . . . and W. Gibson . . . viii, 80 p. front., plates. 19½ᶜᵐ. London and New York, J. Lane, 1904. (*Half-title:* Handbooks of practical gardening. XVIII. Ed. by H. Roberts)   Agr 5—263

Dwyer, Thomas J. Guide to hardy fruits and ornamentals . . . 1 p. l., 125, 1 p. illus. 19½ᶜᵐ. Cornwall, N. Y., T. J. Dwyer & son, 1903.   Agr 5—129

Ferrari, Giovanni Battista. Flora; ouero, cvltvra di fiori . . . Distinta in quattro libri e trasportata dalla lingua latina nell' italiana da Lvdouico Aureli Perugino. 7 p. l., 520, [26] p., 1 l. incl. plates. 23½ᶜᵐ. Roma, P. A. Facciotti, 1638.   Agr 5—311
Added t.-p., engr.

Fischer, Theobald. Der ölbaum. Seine geographische verbreitung, seine wirtschaftliche und kulturhistorische bedeutung . . . 2 p. l., 87, [1] p. fold. map. 28ᶜᵐ. Gotha, J. Perthes, 1904. (Ergänzungsheft no. 147 zu "Petermanns mitteilungen")
      Agr 5—283

Flora and sylva. A monthly review for lovers of garden, woodland, tree or flower; new and rare plants, trees, shrubs, and fruits; the garden beautiful, home woods, and home landscape. Ed. by . . . W. Robinson . . . vol. ii. illus., col. plates. 32½cm. London, 1904.

Die **Gartenwelt**; illustriertes wochenblatt für den gesamten gartenbau, hrsg. von Max Hesdörffer . . . 8. jahrg. (1903–04) illus., plates (partly col.) 30cm. Leipzig, R. C. Schmidt & co., 1904.

Girola, Carlos D. Informe sobre la primera exposición de frutas celebrada en la capital de la República desde 15 de noviembre de 1903 hasta 30 de abril de 1904 . . . 64 p. illus., fold. tab. 26½cm. Buenos Aires, Compañía Sud-Americana de billetes de banco, 1904. (República Argentina. Anales del Ministerio de agricultura. Sección agricultura; botánica y agronomía. Agronomía, tomo iii, no. 1) Agr 5—323

Harrison, C. S. A manual on the propagation and cultivation of the paeony . . . cover-title, 64 p. plates. 23½cm. York, Nebr., Republican [1903?] Agr 5—262

Henderson, **Peter**, **& co.**, pub. Henderson's bulb culture . . . 68 p. illus. 24cm. [New York, P. Henderson & co.] 1904. ' Agr 5—260

Illinois state horticultural society. Transactions . . . for the year 1904, being the proceedings of the 49th annual meeting . . . also proceedings of the Northern, Central and Southern district societies and a number of county societies for the year 1904. new ser. vol. xxxviii. front., illus. (map) plates. 22cm. Springfield, The H. W. Rokker co., printers and binders, 1905.

India—*Mysore*—*Government gardens and parks, Superintendent of.* Annual report . . . for the year 1903–04. With the government review thereon. 33cm. [n. p., 1904]

Jacquin, *aîné.* Monographie complète du melon, contenant la culture, la description et le classement de toutes les variétés de cette espèce, suivies de celles de la pastèque à chair fondante, avec la figure de chacune dessinée et coloriée d'après nature . . . 2 p. 1., iv, 109 p. xxiii col. pl. 22½cm. Paris, Rousselon [etc.] 1832. Bibliography: p. iv. Agr 5—4

Minnesota state horticultural society. Trees, fruits and flowers of Minnesota, 1900–04; embracing the transactions of the Minnesota state horticultural society from December 1, 1893, to December 1, 1904, including . . . the "Minnesota horticulturist" for 1900–04. front., illus., ports., plates. 23½cm. Minneapolis, Harrison & Smith co., printers, 1900–04.

Molnár, István. Magyar pomologia. Vizeki Tallián Béla, M. Kir. földmivelé-sügyi minister megbízásából . . . iii. füzet. Pomologie hongroise. Rédigée par ordre de M. Béla Tellián . . . ministre royal hongrois de l'agriculture . . . iii. livraison. xiii–xviii col. pl. 54½cm. [Budapesten] Az. Athenaeum R.-T. Kö- és könyvnyomdája [1903]

Müller, Johann Georg. Deliciae hortenses. Das ist: blumen-artzney-kuchen-und baum-gartens-lust, in zwey absonderliche theile verfasset. In dem ersten theil wird gelehret wie auffs schönste zu pflantzē: i. Ein blumen-garten . . . ii. Ein artz-ney-garten . . . iii. Ein kuchen-garten . . . In dem andern theil. Ein baum-garten . . . Zu weniger zeit zusamen getragen, nun aber auf begehren auffs neue wider übersehn und mit sehr vielem, wie nach folgende seite ausgeweiset, vermehret. Durch einen besondern liebhaber solches garten-gewåchs. M. J. G. M. . . . 2 pts. in 1 v. front. 13½cm. Stuttgart, J. G. Zubrod, 1676. Agr 5—310

New Zealand—*Agriculture, Dept. of*—*Biology and pomology, Division of.* . . . Twelfth report, 1904. . . . plates. 24cm. Wellington, J. Mackay, government printer, 1904.

North Georgia fruit growers' association. Proceedings of 7th annual session . . . held at Rome, Georgia, May 12, 1904. plates. 23cm. Rome, Rome publishing co., 1904.

Oliver, George W. Plant culture; a working handbook of every day practice for all who grow flowering and ornamental plants in the garden and greenhouse . . . 193 p. 19ᶜᵐ. New York, A. T. De La Mare printing and publishing co., ltd., 1900.

Aug. 16, 1900—110

Powell, Edward Payson. . . . The country home. 5 p. l., 382, [1] p. front., 21 pl. 21ᶜᵐ. New York, McClure, Phillips & co., 1904. (The country home library)

4—37012

Smith, Elmer- D. Smith's chrysanthemum manual. . . . 78 p. illus. 18ᶜᵐ. Adrian, Mich., Finch, the printer, 1904.

Agr 5—259

Southern shippers' guide publishing co. Directory of southern fruit and truck shippers, 1905. 22ᶜᵐ. Houston, Texas [1905]

—— —— Supplement A . . . February 1, 1905. 22½ᶜᵐ. Houston, Texas, 1905.

Utah—*Horticulture, State board of.* Biennial report . . . of the years 1903–1904. illus. 23ᶜᵐ. Salt Lake City, Star printing company, 1905.

Vilmorin, Maurice Lévêque de. Fruticetum Vilmorinianum. Catalogus primarius. Catalogue des arbustes existant en 1904 dans la collection de M. Maurice Lévêque de Vilmorin, avec la description d'espèces nouvelles et de l'introduction récente, par Maurice L. de Vilmorin . . . et D. Bois . . . xvi, 284 p. illus. 28ᶜᵐ. Paris, Librairie agricole [etc.] 1904.

Agr 5—304

Wisconsin state cranberry growers' association. Proceedings of the 18th annual meeting. 22ᶜᵐ. [n. p., 1905]

Wisconsin state horticultural society. Annual report . . . for . . . 1901–04. . . . vol. xxxi–xxxiv. fronts., ports., plates. 22½ᶜᵐ. Madison, Democrat printing co., state printer, 1901–04.

Woburn experimental fruit farm. . . . Fourth report . . .. by the Duke of Bedford, K. G., and Spencer U. Pickering, F. R. S. 21½ᶜᵐ. London, Eyre and Spottiswoode, 1904.

10. FORESTRY.

Alsace-Lorraine—*Finanzen, gewerbe und domänen, Abteilung für.* Beiträge zur forststatistik von Elsass-Lothringen . . . hft. xxii, Wirtschafts- und rechnungsjahr 1903. fold. tables. 24½ᶜᵐ. Strassburg, Im kommissionsverlag der Strassburger druckerei u. verlagsanstalt, 1905.

Cieslar, Adolf. Studien über die qualität rasch erwachsenen fichtenholzes. I. Forstbotanischer theil. Von Dr. A. Cieslar. II. Technologischer theil. Von G. Janka. . . . Mittheilung der K. K. Forstlichen versuchsanstalt in Mariabrunn . . . 69 p. 24½ᶜᵐ. Wien, W. Frick, 1902.

Agr 5—128

Separatabdruck aus dem "Centralblatt für das gesammte forstwesen," hft. 8/9 von 1902.

Croy, Friedrich. Forstliche baukunde. Vorträge über hoch-, weg-, brücken- und wasser-bau . . . 2 p. l., 313, ix p. illus., x pl. (partly col., partly fold.) 26ᶜᵐ. Böhm. Leipa, J. Künster, 1900.

Agr 5—3

A list of works consulted on p. l. 2.

Delassasseigne. . . . Dunes et landes de Gascogne. La défense des forêts contre les incendies . . . 36 p. 27ᶜᵐ. Paris, Imprimerie nationale, 1900.

Agr 5—9

At head of title: République française. Ministère de l'agriculture. Administration des eaux et forêts. Exposition universelle internationale de 1900 à Paris.

English arboricultural society. Transactions . . . vol. vi, pt. i. Comp. by John Davidson . . . plates. 21ᶜᵐ. Carlisle, printed for the Society, 1904–05.

Flagg, Wilson. A year among the trees; or, The woods and by-ways of New England . . . xviii, 335 p. 19½ᶜᵐ. Boston, Estes and Lauriat, 1881.

Agr 5—265

Guyot, Charles. Commentaire de la loi forestière algérienne promulguée le 21 février 1903 . . . xv, 356 p. 23ᶜᵐ. Paris, L. Laveur, 1904.

Agr 5—266

Des **Holzhändlers** forstliches wörterbuch. Was der holzhändler und holzindustrielle vom forstwesen wissen muss . . . Hrsg. vom "Holzmark" -Bunzlau, fachblatt für holzhandel und holzverwertung. 2 p. l., [1], 95 p. illus. 22½ᶜᵐ. Bunzlau, Druck von L. Fernbach, 1903. Agr 5—8

Huffel, G. . . . Économie forestière. Tome I. L'utilité des forêts, propriété et législation forestières, politique forestière, la France forestière, statistiques. 25ᶜᵐ. Paris, L. Laveur, 1904.

India—*Forest dept.* Review of forest administration in British India for the year 1902–03 . . . fold. map. 33½ᶜᵐ. Calcutta, office of the superintendent of government printing, 1904.

India—*Imperial forest school, Dehra Dún.* . . . Calendar. July 1, 1904. tables. 21ᶜᵐ. Calcutta, Office of the superintendent government printing, 1904.

Indiana—*Forestry, State board of.* . . . Fourth annual report . . . 1904. front. illus. 22½ᶜᵐ. Indianapolis, W. B. Burford, printer and binder, [1905]

Jacquot, A. . . . Incendies en forêt.—Évaluation des dommages.—Contentieux.—Mesures préservatrices.—Constatations.—Principes des expertises.—Taux.—Estimation en fonds et superficie.—Trouble d'aménagement.—Préjudices accessoires et indirects.—Spécimens de rapports.—Tarifs.—Etc. . . . 2 éd. 400 p. 25ᶜᵐ. Paris [etc.] Berger-Levrault & cie., 1904. Agr 5—300
"Bibliographie:" p. [13]–23.

Japan—*Agriculture and commerce, Dept. of*—*Forestry, Bureau of.* . . . Forestry and forest-products of Japan. 2 p. l., 118 p. 8 diagr. 22½ᶜᵐ. Tokyo [Printed at the Tokyo Kokubunsha] 1904. 4–31584
At head of title: Universal exposition, Saint Louis, 1904.

Kaiser, Otto. Die wirthschaftliche eintheilung der forsten mit besonderer berücksichtigung des gebirges in verbindung mit der wegenetzlegung . . . vii, 164 p. illus., fold. maps, plans (1 fold.) 24ᶜᵐ. Berlin, J. Springer, 1902. Agr 5—131

Koorders, S. H. . . . Bijdrage no. 10 tot de kennis der boomsoorten op Java, door Dr. S. H. Koorders . . . en Dr. Th. Valeton . . . 26ᶜᵐ. Batavia, G. Kolff & co., 1904. (Mededeelingen uit's Lands plantentuin no. LXVIII.)

Maiden, Joseph Henry. The forest flora of New South Wales . . . pt. XII–XIV. plates. 30½–31ᶜᵐ. Sydney, W. A. Gullick, government printer, 1904.
Pub. by the Forest dept. of New South Wales.

New South Wales—*Lands, Dept. of*—*Forestry branch.* . . . Report . . . for the year 1903. plates. 33½ᶜᵐ. Sydney, W. A. Gullick, government printer, 1904.

Perry, G. W. A treatise on turpentine farming; being a review of natural and artificial obstructions, with their results, in which many erroneous ideas are exploded; with remarks on the best method of making turpentine. viii, [9], 163, [1] p. 19ᶜᵐ. Newbern, N. C., Muse & Davies, 1859. Agr 5—301

Pressler, Max Robert. Forstliche cubirungstafeln. 12 erweiterte aufl. hrsg. von Dr. Max Neumeister . . . viii, 132 p. 24½ᶜᵐ. Wien, M. Perles; [etc., etc.] 1904.

Reynard, J. . . . L'arbre (première série). 19ᶜᵐ. Clermont Ferrand, Typographie et lithographie G. Mont-Louis, 1904.

Schlesischer forst-verein. Jahrbuch . . . für 1904 . . . illus., fold. map. 21½ᶜᵐ. Breslau, E. Morgenstern, 1904.

Schwappach, Adam Friedrich. . . . Forestry, tr. from the German . . . by Fraser Story . . . and Eric A. Nobbs . . . xii, 158 p. illus. 15½ᶜᵐ. [London, Aldine house, J. M. Dent & Co., 1904] (The Temple primers) Agr 5—121
Added illus. t.-p.

South Australia—*Woods and forests dept.* Annual progress report upon state forest administration . . . for the year 1903–4. plates. 33½ᶜᵐ. Adelaide, C. E. Bristow, government printer, 1904.

Transvaal—*Forests, Conservator of.* Transvaal forest report, by D. E. Hutchins. . . . 24½ᶜᵐ. Pretoria, printed at the government printing and stationery office, 1904. .

Turskiĭ, M[itrofan Kuz'mich] Liesovodstvo . . . 3-ᵉizdanie. VIII, 377 p. illus., map, plans (1 fold.) 27ᶜᵐ. Moskva, Tipo-litografiia T-va I. N. Kushnerev i ko., 1904. Agr 5—133
Sylviculture.

Victorian exhibition, 1861. . . . Report on class III. Indigenous vegetable substances. .. 61 p. 21ᶜᵐ. Melbourne, J. Ferres, government printer, 1862. [*With* Lawes, Sir John B. Agricultural chemistry. On the growth of barley. London, ·1858]

Ward, Harry Marshall. Trees; a handbook of forest botany for the woodlands and the laboratory . . . vol. i-ii. fronts., illus. 19ᶜᵐ. Cambridge, At the University press, 1904. (*Half-title:* Cambridge biological series)
CONTENTS.—vol. I. Buds and twigs.—vol. II. Leaves.

11. DOMESTIC ANIMALS.

American Aberdeen-Angus breeders' association. The American Aberdeen-Angus herd-book, containing a record of Aberdeen-Angus cattle . . . v. 12–13. 26ᶜᵐ. Davenport, Iowa, Egbert, Fidlar & Chambers, printers, 1902–04.

American Berkshire association. American Berkshire record . . . vol. XXII–XXIII. 24ᶜᵐ. Springfield, Ill., 1904–05.

American Galloway breeders' association. The American Galloway herd book, containing pedigrees of pure-bred Galloway cattle . . . vol. XIV. front., plates. 22½ᶜᵐ. Cedar Rapids, Iowa, Press of Republican printing co., 1904.

American Poland-China record. The American Poland-China record . . . vol. XXXV–XXXVI. 23½ᶜᵐ. Columbia, Mo., Press of E. W. Stephens, 1904–05.

American saddle-horse breeders' association. The register . . . vol. v. 23½ᶜᵐ. Louisville, Kentucky, Press of the Bradley & Gilbert company, 1904.

American short-horn breeders' association. . . . The American short-horn herd book. (new series) v. 58–59. 23½ᶜᵐ. Chicago, American short-horn breeders' association, 1904.

American society for the prevention of cruelty to animals. . . . Thirty-ninth annual report for the year ending December 31, 1904. front., plates. 22ᶜᵐ. New York, 1905.

American Suffolk flock register association. The American Suffolk sheep record . . . vol. I. front. 23ᶜᵐ. Des Moines, Ia., Published by the American Suffolk flock register association [190–]

Argentine Republic—*Agricultura, Ministerio de—Agricultura y ganadería, Dirección de.* . . . Feria exposición de ganadería celebrada por la Sociedad rural Argentina en el mes de septiembre de 1901 . . . illus., col. pl. 26½ᶜᵐ. Buenos Aires, Talleres de publicaciones de la Oficina meteorológica Argentina, 1903. (República Argentina. Anales del ministerio de agricultura. Sección de zootecnia, bacteriología veterinaria y zoología. Tomo I, núm. 2.) Agr 5—317

Ayrshire breeders' association. The Ayrshire record. new ser., vol. VIII, X, XII, XV. American and Canadian Ayrshire herd record (old ser., vol. XII, XIV, XVI, XIX). 23½ᶜᵐ. Albany, The Argus company, printers, 1891–1904.

Ayrshire breeders' association. · Year book of the Ayrshire breeders for the year 1904. Containing the proceedings of the annual meeting, recent milk and butter records, and general information about Ayrshires and the Ayrshire breeders' association. front., plates. 20½ᶜᵐ. [Brandon, Vt., Brandon publishing company, 1904]

Battell, Joseph. The Morgan horse and register, containing the history and pedigree of Justin Morgan, founder of this remarkable American breed of horses, and of his best known sons and grandsons . . . vol. I. front. (double tab.) plates, port., double map. 26½ᶜᵐ. Middlebury, Vt., Register printing company, 1894.

Black top Spanish merino sheep breeders' publishing association. The black top Spanish merino sheep register . . . vol. v. front., plates. 23ᶜᵐ. Washington, Pa., H. F. Ward, printer and binder, 1901.

Brown, Edward. Poultry-keeping as an industry for farmers and cottagers . . . 5th ed., rev. and enl. viii, 205 p. incl. front., illus. 25ᶜᵐ. London, E. Arnold [1904].

Brown Swiss cattle breeders' association. The Swiss record (continued from vol. II) supplement no. 4 . . . 23ᶜᵐ. Owego, N. Y., Printed at the Times office, 1904.

Chicago, Union stock yard and transit company of. . . . Thirty-ninth annual live stock report for 1904 and summary for years 1865 to 1904. 17ᶜᵐ. [Chicago, The Union stock yard and transit co., 1905]

Chicago daily drovers' journal. "Our year book," telling tables of the live stock trade for the year 1904. With general information, including monthly and yearly comparisons for a term of years. 18½ᶜᵐ. Chicago, Chicago daily drovers' journal [1905]

Cover-title reads: Year book of figures relating to the live stock business.

Coates's herd book: containing the pedigrees of improved shorthorn cattle. v. 50 (new ser.) . . . 21½ᶜᵐ. London and Beccles, W. Clowes and sons, limited, 1904.

Collingwood, Herbert Winslow, *ed.* The business hen (a new brood). Herbert W. Collingwood, ed.; assisted by Prof. James E. Rice, Miss F. E. Wheeler . . . and many others. 125, [1] p. illus., diagrs. 19½ᶜᵐ. New York, The Rural New Yorker [1904]

4—28219

Compton, Herbert Eastwick. The twentieth century dog . . . comp. from the contributions of over five hundred experts . . . 2 v. illus., 82 pl. (incl. col. fronts.) 21½ᶜᵐ. London, G. Richards, 1904.   Agr 5—136
CONTENTS.—I. Non-sporting.—II. Sporting.

Devon longwoolled sheep breeders' society. The flock book of Devon longwoolled sheep. vol. III. With supplement 1902 and 1903 . . . 22ᶜᵐ. Taunton, E. Goodman & son, Phœnix printing works, 1904.

Friesch rundvee-stamboek. Hulp-stamboek 1905. aflevering xix. fold. pl. 19½ᶜᵐ. Leeuwarden, N. Miedema & co., 1905.

Friesch rundvee-stamboek; verzamelboek van het stamboekvee en de afstammelingen bij ieder der leden aanwezig op 12 november 1904. 19½ᶜᵐ. Leeuwarden, N. Miedema & co., 1905.

Galloway cattle society. The Galloway herd book, containing pedigrees of pure-bred Galloway cattle . . . vol. xxv. front. (port.) 22½ᶜᵐ. Dumfries, Printed at the Courier and Herald offices, 1905.

Goldbeck, Paul. Zucht und remontirung der militärpferde aller staaten. ix, 415, [1] p. fold. tables. 24½ᶜᵐ. Berlin, E. S. Mittler und sohn, 1901.   Agr 5—14
"Litteratur" at the end of each section.

Gt. Brit.—*Admiralty—Committee on humane slaughtering of animals.* . . . Report of the committee appointed by the Admiralty to consider the humane slaughtering of animals, with appendix . . . 26 p. plates (partly fold.) 33ᶜᵐ. London, Printed for H. M. Stationery off., by Wyman and sons, limited, 1904.   Agr 5—137

Inland poultry journal, a monthly journal of reliable poultry information. Feb. 1902–Jan. 1903. vol. vi, no. x—vol. viii, no. 1. illus. 28½ᶜᵐ. Indianapolis, 1902–03.

Kennel club. The Kennel club calendar and stud book. The only record published in England of dog shows and field trials for the year 1904 . . . vol. xxxii. 20½ᶜᵐ. London, Published for the Kennel club at the "Field" office, 1905.

Lassmann, Ferdinand. Massnahmen zur hebung der rindvieh-, schweine- und ziegenzucht, nebst anhang: Statistische daten und vergleiche aus der viehzählung vom jahre 1890. und 1900 . . . 93 p. fold. pl., fold. maps, xi fold. tab. 26ᶜᵐ. Prag, Verlag der Deutschen sektión des Landeskulturrates für das königreich Böhmen, 1904. (*On cover:* Arbeiten der Deutschen sektion des Landeskulturrates für das königreich Böhmen. hft. viii)   Agr 5—12
"Massnahmen zur hebung der schweinezucht von Josef Wozak."

Lassmann, Ferdinand. Zur hebung der rindviehzucht im Böhmerwalde. Vorschläge der Deutschen sektion des Landesculturrathes für das königreich Böhmen und hierauf fussende massnahmen des K. K. Ackerbauministeriums und des Landesausschusses des königreiches Böhmen. 37 p. double map. 26ᶜᵐ. Prag, Verlag der Deutschen section des Landesculturrathes für das königreich Böhmen, 1902. (*On cover:* Arbeiten der Deutschen section des Landesculturrathes für das königreich Böhmen. hft. v) .   Agr 5—124

Lydtin, August. Rechenknecht. Anleitung für den praktischen landwirt zur gewinnung von vergleichenden zahlen der an rindern und pferden genommenen körpermasse . . . 1 p. l., xxi p., 1 l., 147, [1] p. incl. tables. 17½ᶜᵐ. Karlsruhe, Macklot'sche druckerei [1896] (*Added t.-p.:* Anleitung für den praktischen landwirt. Hrsg. vom direktorium der Deutschen landwirtschafts-gesellschaft. Der sammlung nr. 7)   Agr 5—270

Manitoba—*Agriculture and immigration, Dept. of.* Reports of the live stock associations and the Dairy association for the year 1904. 25ᶜᵐ. Winnipeg, 1904.

The **Meat** trades journal and cattle salesman's gazette . . . January 7th, 1904– December 29th, 1904. [v. 19–20] 37½ᶜᵐ. London, Meat trades journal printing & publishing company, limited [1904]

National association of wool manufacturers. . . . Annual wool review 1904; domestic wool clip, imports of wool and woolens and other statistical tables. fold. tables. 23½ᶜᵐ. Boston, The Rockwell and Churchill press, 1904.

National association of wool manufacturers. Bulletin . . . 1904. front., illus., ports., fold. map, fold. tab. 23½ᶜᵐ. Boston, Mass., 1904.

National delaine merino sheep breeders' association. Delaine merino register . . . vol. vii. 22½ᶜᵐ. Canonsburg, Pa., J. G. Charlton, printer, 1904.

National live stock association. Proceedings of the National stock growers' convention and organization of the National live stock association of the United States, Denver, Colo., January 25, 26, 27. Published by the Denver chamber of commerce and board of trade, and presented to the National live stock association, with an appendix embracing the latest information on the resources of the city of Denver . . . front, ports. 23ᶜᵐ. Denver, News job printing, 1898.

New York state American sheep breeders' association. Register . . . vol. iii. 22½ᶜᵐ. Rochester, N. Y., Artistic printing and engraving co., 1898.

O. I. C. swine breeders' association. The O. I. C. swine breeders' association record . . . v. 7. front. 24ᶜᵐ. [n. p.] 1905.

Ohio Poland-China record company. The Ohio Poland-China record . . . vol. xxv. port. 24ᶜᵐ. Dayton, Press of the Western printing and publishing company, 1903.

Ontario, Live stock associations of the province of. Annual reports . . . 1903 . . . 25ᶜᵐ. Toronto, Printed by L. K. Cameron, printer to the king's most excellent Majesty, 1904.

Plumb, Charles Sumner. Little sketches of famous beef cattle . . .   99 p. 21½ x 12^{cm}. Columbus, O., The author, 1904.   4—16213

Red-polled cattle club, of America. The red-polled herd book of cattle descended from the Norfolk & Suffolk red polled. American ser. vol. XVI. 23½^{cm}. [n. p.] Published by the Red-polled cattle club of America, 1904.

Rice, William Edward. The Feather's practical squab book. Questions and answers . . . 112 p. illus. 23^{cm}. Washington, G. E. Howard [1904].   Agr 5—272

Rundvee stamboek "Noord-Holland." aflevering XIII; 1903–04. 21½^{cm}. Hoorn, Stoomdruk, Geerts & Kops, 1904.

St. Louis. Louisiana purchase exposition—*Press and publicity, Committee on.* Official catalogue of exhibitors . . . Dept. R. Live stock . . . Rev. ed. 5 pts. 23^{cm} (pt. 3, 22½^{cm}) St. Louis, Official catalogue company (inc.) 1904.
CONTENTS.—[pt. 1] Div. A. Horses, asses, and mules. Div. B. Cattle.—[pt. 2] Div. C. Sheep. Div. D. Swine.—[pt. 3] Div. E. Poultry, pigeons, and pet stock.—[pt. 4] Div. F. Dogs.—[pt. 5] Div. G. Southern breeding cattle.

Shaw, Thomas. The feeding and management of live stock. A series of lectures . . . 2d ed. 99 p. 21^{cm}. St. Anthony Park, Minnesota [Webb publishing co., 1902]   Agr 5—94

Shaw, Thomas. Sheep husbandry in Minnesota . . . 2d ed. . . . 5 p. l., [9]–213 p. front., illus. 18½^{cm}. St. Paul, Webb publishing co., 1901. .   5—2406

Standard Poland-China record association. The standard Poland-China record . . . vol. XVIII. 23^{cm}. Maryville, Mo., Press of the Nodaway democrat, 1904.

Sweden—*Kongl. landtbruksstyrelse.* Riksstambok öfver Ayrshire-boskap . . . I–II delen. 29^{cm}. Malmö, Förlags-aktiebolagets boktryckeri, 1904.
I. del in 3 pts, and Register.

Wallace's American trotting register, containing the pedigrees of standard bred trotters and pacers and an appendix of non-standard animals. vol. XVI. 24^{cm}. Chicago, American trotting register association, 1904.

Wallace's year-book of trotting and pacing in 1903–04 . . . vol. XIX–XX. 24^{cm}. Chicago, American trotting register association, 1904–05.

Welsh pony and cob society. The Welsh pony and cob stud book . . . vol. I–III. plates. 22^{cm}. Hereford, Printed for the society at the offices of the "Hereford times," 1902–04.

Western trunk line association. . . . Quarantine rules and regulations of the United States department of agriculture, the various states and territories, the republic of Mexico and the dominion of Canada. Applying on state and interstate traffic . . . Amendment no. 15. 26½ x 21½^{cm}. Chicago, W. J. Hartman co., printers and binders, 1905. (Joint circular W. T. L. no. 72)

12. FEEDING OF ANIMALS.

Cugini, Gino. . . . La conservazione dei foraggi allo stato fresco . . . 2. ed. riveduta ed ampliata dall' autore. x, 190 p. illus., fold. diagr. 19^{cm}. Casale, Tipografia e litografia C. Cassone, 1901. (*On cover:* Biblioteca agraria Ottavi, vol. XVII)   Agr 5—295
"Elenco di pubblicazioni riguardanti la conservazione dei foraggi verdi mediante l'infossamento e la compressione": p. 168–190.

Lawes, *Sir* John Bennet, *1st bart.* Fifth report of experiments on the feeding of sheep. By J. B. Lawes . . . & Dr. J. H. Gilbert . . . 14 p., 11. 21^{cm}. London, Printed by W. Clowes and sons, 1861. [*With his* Agricultural chemistry. On the growth of barley. London, 1858]
"From the Journal of the Royal agricultural society of England, vol. XXII, pt. I."

Lawes, *Sir* John Bennet, *1st bart.* Report of experiments on the fattening of oxen at Woburn Park farm. By J. B. Lawes . . . & Dr. J. H. Gilbert . . . 20 p. 21ᶜᵐ. London, Printed by W. Clowes and sons, 1861. [*With his* Agricultural chemistry. On the growth of barley. London, 1858]
"From the Journal of the Royal agricultural society of England, vol. XXII, pt. I.

Stefánsson, Stefán. . . . Isländska foder- och betesväxter II, af Stefán Stefánsson och H. G. Söderbaum. 24ᶜᵐ. Stockholm, P. A. Norstedt & söner, 1904. (Meddelanden från Kungl. landtbruks-akademiens experimentalfält, n:o 83.)
"Aftryck ur Kungl. landtbruks-akademiens handlingar och tidskrift för år 1904.

Tangl, Franz, *ed.* Beiträge zur futtermittellehre und stoffwechselphysiologie der landwirtschaftlichen nutztiere . . . 1. hft. 25½ᶜᵐ. Berlin, P. Parey, 1905.

Voelcker, John Christopher Augustus. The changes which take place in the field and stack in haymaking. By Dr. Augustus **V**oelcker. 32 p. 21½ᶜᵐ. London, Printed by W. Clowes and sons, 1867. [*With his* On milk. London, 1863]
"From the Journal of the Royal agricultural society of England, vol. III.—S. S., pt. I."

Voelcker, John Christopher Augustus. On the composition and nutritive value of palm-nut kernal [!] meal and cake. 7 p. 21½ᶜᵐ. London, Printed by W. Clowes and sons, 1865. [*With his* On milk. London, 1863]
"From the Journal of the Royal agricultural society of England, S. S.—vol. I, pt. I."

13. VETERINARY MEDICINE.

Behring, Emil Adolph von, *ed.* Beiträge zur experimentellen therapie . . . hft. 9. v pl. (4 fold.) 25ᶜᵐ. Berlin, A. Hirschwald, 1905.
CONTENTS.—I. Schutzimpfungsversuche gegen die tuberculose der rinder nach v. Behring's methode. Von Dr. Franz Hutyra . . .—II. Weitere studien zur frage der intrauterinen und extrauterinen antitoxinübertragung von der mutter auf ihre nachkommen. Von Dr. Paul H. Römer . . .

Cadéac, C. . . . Sémiologie et diagnostic des maladies des animaux domestiques . . . 2 v. illus. 18ᶜᵐ. . 2. éd. . . . Paris, J.-B. Baillière et fils, 1905. (*Half-title:* Encyclopédie Cadéac. II–III)   Agr 5—135
At head of title: Encyclopédie vétérinaire pub. sous la direction de C. Cadéac.

Hayes, M. Horace. Veterinary notes for horse owners. A manual of horse medicine and surgery, written in popular language . . . 6th ed., rev., enl. . . . xxiv, 828 p. incl. front., illus. 21ᶜᵐ. London, Hurst and Blackett, limited, 1903.
                        Agr 5—93

Jahresbericht über die verbreitung von tierseuchen im Deutschen reiche . . . 14.–18. jahrg., 1899–1903. fold. maps. 28ᶜᵐ. Berlin, J. Springer, 1900–04.

Leblanc, P. The diseases of the mammary gland of the domestic animals . . . Authorised tr. by Lieutenant-Colonel J. A. Nunn . . . xii, 111 p. illus. 25ᶜᵐ. London, Baillière, Tindall and Cox, 1904.   Agr 5—251

14. DAIRY.

Evans, James Rittenhouse. A laboratory handbook for the analysis of milk, butter, and cheese . . . 48 p. 17½ᶜᵐ. [n. p., 1904]   Agr 5—75

France—*Agriculture, Ministère de l'—Renseignements agricoles, Office de—Études techniques, Service des.* . . . Enquête sur l'industrie laitière. tome 1. fold. map. 28ᶜᵐ. Paris, Imprimerie nationale, 1903.

Iowa—*Dairy commissioner.* Eighteenth annual report . . . for the year 1904 . . . 22½ᶜᵐ. Des Moines, B. Murphy, state printer, 1904.

Netherlands—*Waterstaat, handel en nijverheid, Departement van—Afdeeling landbouw* . . . Mededeelingen van consulaire ambtenaren over nederlandsche kaas. 111 p. 24½ᶜᵐ. 's-Gravenhage [Gedrukt bij Gebrs. J. & H. van Langenhuysen] 1904. (Verslagen en mededeelingen van de Afdeeling landbouw van het Departement van waterstaat, handel en nijverheid. 1904, no. 5)

Voelcker, John Christopher Augustus. · Cheese experiments . . . 23 p. 21½^{cm}. London, Printed by W. Clowes and sons, 1862. [*With his* On milk. London, 1863] "From the Journal of the Royal agricultural society of England, vol. XXIII."

Voelcker, John Christopher Augustus. Lecture on milk . . . Delivered at the weekly council meeting of the Royal agricultural society, March 12, 1862. 12 p. 21½^{cm}. London, Printed by W. Clowes and sons, 1862. [*With his* On milk. London, 1863] "From the Journal of the Royal agricultural society of England, vol. XXIII."

Voelcker, John Christopher Augustus. On milk . . . 37 p. illus. 21½^{cm}. London, Printed by W. Clowes and sons, 1863.   Agr 5—600 "From the Journal of the Royal agricultural society of England, vol. XXIV, pt. II."

Voelcker, John Christopher Augustus. On poisonous cheese . . . 7 p. 21½^{cm}. London, Printed by W. Clowes and sons, 1862. [*With his* On milk. London, 1863] "From the Journal of the Royal agricultural society of England, vol. XXIII."

Voelcker, John Christopher Augustus. On ·the composition of cheese and on practical mistakes in cheese-making . . . 43 p. 21^{cm}. London, Printed by W. Clowes and sons, 1861. [*With* Lawes, Sir John B. Agricultural chemistry. On the growth of barley. London, 1858]   Agr 5—596 "From the Journal of the Royal agricultural society of England, vol. XXII, pt. I."

Wisconsin dairymen's association. Thirty-second annual report . . . 1904. 23^{cm}. Madison, Democrat printing co., state printer, 1904.

15. METEOROLOGY.

Gt. Brit.—*Admiralty.* Rainfall chart of the world. 75 x 126^{cm}. London, Published at the Admiralty, 1874.

Gt. Brit.—*Meteorological council.* Report . . . for the year ending 31st March, 1904, to the president and council of the Royal society . . . front., fold. maps. 24½^{cm}. London, Printed for H. M. Stationery off., by Darling & son, ltd., 1904.

Philippine Islands—*Weather bureau.* Report . . . for the year ended September 1, 1903 . . . plates. 23^{cm}. [Manila, 1903] From the 4th annual report of the Philippine commission.

16. CHEMISTRY AND CHEMICAL TECHNOLOGY.

Argentine Republic—*Comisión de investigación vinícola.* . . . Investigación vinícola complementaria de 1904. 201 p. diagrs. 26½^{cm}. Buenos Aires, Impr. de M. Biedma é hijo, 1904. (República Argentina. Anales del ministerio de agricultura. Sección de comercio, industrias y economía, tomo II)   Agr 5—542

Clowes, Frank. A treatise on practical chemistry and qualitative analysis adapted for use in the laboratories of colleges and schools . . . 7th ed. xxii, 516 p. double front., illus. 19½^{cm}. London, J. & A. Churchill, 1899.   Agr 5—102

Cohn, Lassar. Chemistry in daily life; popular lectures, by Dr. Lassar-Cohn . . . tr. by M. M. Pattison Muir . . 3d ed., rev. and augm. xii, 340 p. illus. 19^{cm}. London, H. Grevel & co., 1905.

Deutsch-amerikanischer techniker-verband. Verbands-statuten und mitglieder-listen . . . 15^{cm}. [New York, The Technical press] 1904.

Essex county, *Eng.*—*Education committee*—*Technical laboratories.* . . . Notes on agricultural analyses, made in the County technical laboratories, Chelmsford, 1901–03, by T. S. Dymond, F. I. C., & F. Hughes. 21½^{cm}. [n. p., 1904]

Hurst, George H. The painter's laboratory guide: a handbook on paints, colours, and varnishes for students . . . ix, [1], 248 p. illus. 20^{cm}. London, C. Griffin and company, limited, 1902.   Agr 5—103

Insurance engineering experiment station, *Boston, Mass.* . . . Report no. xv . . . 27½x21ᶜᵐ. Boston, 1904.
CONTENTS.—Bog fuel, briquettes, coke, and gas. Third report on laboratory tests.

Leavitt, Thomas Hooker. Facts about peat, peat fuel, and peat coke; how to make it and how to use it; what it costs and what it is worth; with brief notes concerning its use and value for numerous other purposes . . . 115 p. 10 pl. 19ᶜᵐ. Boston, Lee and Shepard, 1904·   4—3933

Meunier, Louis. . . . Contribution à l'étude des composés diazoamidés . . . 99 p., 1 l. 25ᶜᵐ. Lyon, A. Rey; [etc., etc.] 1904. (Annales de l'Université de Lyon. Nouv. sér. ɪ. Sciences, médecine. fasc. 13)   Agr 5—104

Owens college, *Manchester, Eng.* Studies from the physical and chemical laboratories . . . vol. ɪ. Physics and physical chemistry. illus. 24½ᶜᵐ. Manchester, Guardian printing works, 1893.

Siena—*Laboratorio chimico municipale.* . . . Rendiconto . . . durante l' anno 1904. 26ᶜᵐ. Siena, Tipografia cooperativa, 1905.

Simmersbach, O. The chemistry of coke: founded on the "Grundlagen der koks-chemie" of O. Simmersbach. 2d ed. Rev. and enl. by W. Carrick Anderson . . . iv p., 2 l., 201, [1] p. fold. tab. 19ᶜᵐ. Glasgow and Edinburg, W. Hodge & co., 1904.   Agr 5—105

Society for the encouragement of arts, manufactures, & commerce—*Committee on the deterioration of paper.* . . . Report . . . With two appendixes: 1. Abstracts of papers on German official tests, 1885–96. 2. Précis of correspondence. 1 p. l., 42 p. 25ᶜᵐ. London, Printed by W. Trounce, 1898.   Agr 5—327

Stolle, F. Handbuch für zuckerfabriks-chemiker. Methoden und vorschriften für die untersuchung von rohprodukten, erzeugnissen und hilfsprodukten der zuckerindustrie . . . xix, 583, [1] p. illus. 22ᶜᵐ. Berlin, P. Parey, 1904.   Agr 5—

Webster, Ralph Waldo. A laboratory manual of physiological chemistry, by Ralph W. Webster . . . and Waldemar Koch . . . vii, 107 p. illus. 23ᶜᵐ. Chicago, The University of Chicago press; London, W. Wesley & son, 1903.   3—16053
Interleaved.

17. FOOD.

Albrand, Walter. Die kostordnung an heil- und pflege-anstalten. Zum gebrauch für ärzte, verwaltungsbeamte, etc. . . . 79 p. 19ᶜᵐ. Leipzig, H. Hartung & sohn, 1903.   Agr 5—268

Atkinson, Amy. . . . Practical cookery. A collection of reliable recipes, comp. by Amy Atkinson and Grace Holroyd . . . with an introduction on cookery by gas . . . [3d ed.] 202, vi p. 19ᶜᵐ. Leeds, Nutt & Co., 1903.   Agr 5—106

Ayr (*England*) district asylum. Thirty-third annual report . . . 1902–3. 21½ᶜᵐ. Ayr, Printed by Ferguson & Coy, 1904.
Contains dietary table.

Benedict, A. L. Practical dietetics . . . 383 p. 19½ᶜᵐ. Chicago, G. P. Engelhard & company, 1904.

Chittenden, Russell Henry. Physiological economy in nutrition, with special reference to the minimal proteid requirement of the healthy man; an experimental study . . . xi p., 1 l., 478 p. 16 pl. 23ᶜᵐ. New York, F. A. Stokes company, 1904.   4—32209

Fulton, E. G. Substitutes for flesh foods; vegetarian cook book . . . 266 p. 18½ᶜᵐ. Oakland, Cal., Pacific press publishing company [1904]   4—11554

Pattee, Alida Frances. Practical dietetics, with reference to diet in disease . . . 2d ed., rev. and enl. xvi, 340 p. illus. 19ᶜᵐ. New York, The author [1904]
Advertising matter. p. 312–340.   4—32689

Prato, Katharina, *edle von Scheiger.* Die süddeutsche küche. Für anfängerinnen und praktische köchinnen zusammengestellt . . . Bereichert und hrsg. von deren enkelin Viktorine von Leitmaier . . . 36., abermals verb. und verm. aufl. . . . viii, 800 p. illus., plates (partly double, partly col.) 22^{cm}. Graz, Verlagsbuchhandlung "Styria," 1904. Agr 5—74

Smedley, Emma. Institution recipes in use at the Johns Hopkins hospital and Drexel institute lunch room . . . 1 p. l., 5–121 p. 19$\frac{1}{2}$^{cm}. Philadelphia, W. F. Fell company, printers [1904]. 4—11212
Sixteen blank pages at end of book for additional recipes.

Vandevelde, A. J. J. . . . Répertoire des travaux publiés sur la composition, l'analyse et les falsifications des denrées alimentaires pendant l'année 1903, par le Dr. A.-J. J. Vandevelde . . . avec la collaboration du Dr. M. Henseval . . . (4e année) 24^{cm}. Bruxelles, Typographie et lithographie A. Lesigne, 1904.
Extrait du Bulletin du Service de surveillance de la fabrication et du commerce des denrées alimentaires (année 1904)

18. MEDICINE, HYGIENE, AND PHYSIOLOGY.

Archiv für die gesammte physiologie des menschen und der thiere. Hrsg. von Dr. E. F. W. Pflüger . . . 1.–34. bd. illus., plates (partly fold., partly col.) 24^{cm}. Bonn, E. Strauss [etc.] 1868–84.

Bender hygienic laboratory. Studies from the Bender hygienic laboratory, Albany, N. Y. Reprints. v. I. front., plates (partly col.), ports. 23^{cm}. Albany, Fort Orange press, 1904.

Coles, Alfred C. Clinical diagnostic bacteriology, including serum diagnosis and cytodiagnosis . . . viii, 237 p., 1 l. illus., II col. pl. 23^{cm}. London, J. & A. Churchill, 1904. Agr 5—95

Connecticut—*Health, State board of.* . . . Twenty-seventh annual report . . . for the year 1904 . . . tables, diagrs. 23$\frac{1}{2}$^{cm}. New Haven, The Tuttle, Morehouse & Taylor company, 1905.

Encyklopädie der hygiéne, hrsg. von Prof. R. Pfeiffer . . . Prof. B. Proskauer . . . unter mitwirkung von Dr. phil. et med. Carl Oppenheimer . . . lfg. 21–23. 28^{cm}. Leipzig, F. C. W. Vogel, 1904.

France—*Hygiène publique, Comité consultatif d'.* . . . Recueil des travaux du Comité consultatif d'hygiène publique de France et des actes officiels de l'administration sanitaire. tome 32 (année 1902) 23^{cm}. Melun, Imprimerie administrative, 1904.

Green, Frederick William Edridge-. Colour-blindness and colour-perception . . . viii, 311, [1] p., incl. diagrs. III col. pl. (incl. front.) 19^{cm}. London, K. Paul, Trench, Trübner & co., ltd., 1891. (*Half-title:* The International scientific ser. vol. LXXI.) Agr 5—331

Kliegl bros. The actinolite for the treatment of disease by actinic light; with the recent literature of actino-therapeusis. 2d ed. 1 p. l., 60 p. illus. 20$\frac{1}{2}$^{cm}. New York, Kliegl bros., 1903.

Laveran, Alphonse, *i. e.,* Charles Louis Alphonse. Trypanosomes et trypanosomiases, par A. Laveran . . . et F. Mesnil . . . xi, 417, [1] p., 1 l. illus., col. pl. 25$\frac{1}{2}$^{cm}. Paris, Masson et c^{ie}, 1904. Agr 5—99

London—*County council—Medical officer of health.* . . . Report of the public health committee . . . submitting the report of the medical officer of health of the county for the year 1903. diagrs. (1 fold.) fold. map. 33^{cm}. London, Printed by J. Truscott and son, ltd., 1904.

Owens college, *Manchester, Eng.* Studies from the physiological laboratory . . . vol. I. illus., plates (partly double, partly fold.) 24½^{cm}. Manchester, J. E. Cornish, 1891.

Queensland—*Hydraulic engineer.* . . . Twentieth annual report . . . on water supply. fold. map. 34½^{cm}. [Brisbane, G. A. Vaughn, government printer, 1904]

Thresh, John C. The examination of waters and water supplies . . . xvi, 460 p. incl. xix pl., diagrs. 24^{cm}. Philadelphia, P. Blakiston's son & co., 1904. Agr 5—326

Voelcker, John Christopher Augustus. Lecture on town sewage . . . Delivered at the weekly council meeting of the Royal agricultural society, May 28, 1862. 11, [1] p. 21½^{cm}. London, Printed by W. Clowes and sons, 1862. [*With his* On milk. London, 1863.]

"From the Journal of the Royal agricultural society of England, vol. XXIII."

19. PHARMACY.

The **British** and colonial druggist's diary 1905. 28½^{cm}. [London, 1905]

Gautier, Armand *i. e.* Émile Julien Armand. Les alcaloïdes de l'huile de foie de morue, par Armand Gautier . . . et L. Mourgues . . . 43 p., 1 l. 24½^{cm}. Paris, G. Masson, 1890. Agr 5—78

Haarlem, Kolonial museum te. Bulletin . . . no. 32; februari, 1905. Inhoud: Bijdragen tot de kennis van het gebruik van sirih in Nederlandsch-Oost-Indië . . . illus., plates. 22½^{cm}. Amsterdam, Uitgave van het Museum, 1905.

Lohmann, C. E. Julius. Über die giftigkeit der deutschen schachtelhalmarten, insbesondere des duwocks (Equisetum palustre) . . . 4 p. l., 69 p. ii pl. 24^{cm}. Berlin, Deutsche landwirtschafts-gesellschaft, 1904. (*Added t.-p.:* Arbeiten der Deutschen landwirtschafts-gesellschaft . . . hft. 100) Agr 5—115
Plates accompanied by guard sheet with description.

New York state pharmaceutical association. Proceedings of the 24th annual meeting . . . held at Elmira, New York, June 24th, 25th, 26th and 27th, 1902 . . . 22½^{cm}. Elmira, The Advertiser association press [1902]

Perrot, Émile. Cartes de distribution géographique des principales matières premières d'origine végétale, dressées sur les indications de M. Émile Perrot . . . par H. Frouin . . . fold. maps. 24^{cm}. Paris, A. Joanin et c^{ie} [1904] Agr 5—31

20. PALEONTOLOGY AND GEOLOGY.

Argentine Republic—*Agricultura, Ministerio de.* . . . Anales . . . Sección geología, mineralogía y minería, tomo I, núm. 1. Informe sobre máquinas perforadoras. Carbón, petróleo y agua en la République Argentina. Reconocimiento geológico del territorio de Misiones. illus., fold. plates, fold. maps. 26½^{cm}. Buenos Aires, Talleres de publicaciones de la Oficina meteorológica argentina, 1904.

Baier, Johann Jakob. Oruktographia norica, sive Rervm fossilivm et ad minerale regnvm pertinentivm, in territorio norimbergensi ejvsqve vicinia observatarvm svccincta descriptio . . . 3 p. l., 102, [2] p. vi fold. pl. 21 x 16½^{cm}. Norimbergæ, impensis W. Michahellis, 1708. [*With* Volckamer, Johann G. Flora noribergensis. Norimbergæ, 1700]

Baier, Johann Jakob. . . . Sciagraphia mvsei svi accedvnt svpplementa Oryctographiæ noricæ . . . 1 p. l., 64, [2] p. iii pl. (1 fold.) 21 x 16½^{cm}. Norimbergæ, apvd hæredes W. M. Endteri et I. A. Engelbrechti vidvam, 1730. [*With* Volckamer, Johann G. Flora noribergensis. Norimbergæ, 1700]

Ball, Sir Robert Stawell. The cause of an ice age . . . 2d ed. xv, 180 p: front., illus. 19½^{cm}. London, K. Paul, Trench, Trübner & co., ltd., 1892. (*Half-title:* Modern science ed. by Sir John Lubbock [1]) Agr 5—330

Canada—*Geological survey.* Annual report, vol. xiv, pt. H . . . Report on the origin, geological relations and composition of the nickel and copper deposits of the Sudbury mining district, Ontario, Canada, by Alfred Ernest Barlow . . . plates, fold. maps in case. 25ᶜᵐ. Ottawa, Printed by S. E. Dawson, printer to the king's most excellent Majesty, 1904.

Georgia—*Geological survey.* . . . Bulletin. no. 11–12. fronts., illus., plates (partly fold.) 25½ᶜᵐ. [Atlanta, G. W. Harrison, state printer] 1904.
CONTENTS.—no. 11, Watson, T. L. A preliminary report on the bauxite deposits of Georgia.—no. 12, McCallie, S. W. A preliminary report on the coal deposits of Georgia.

Jahrbuch für das berg- und hüttenwesen im königreiche Sachsen. Jahrg. 1904 (Statistik vom jahre 1903) . . . illus., v pl. (3 fold. & col.) 25ᶜᵐ. Freiberg, Craz & Gerlach (J. Stettner) [n. d.]

New York (*state*)—*Museum.* . . . Bulletin 77. Geology 6. Geology of the vicinity of Little Falls, Herkimer county, by H. P. Cushing . . . illus., 16 pl. (1 fold.) 2 fold. maps in pocket. 23ᶜᵐ. Albany, New York state education dept., 1905.

Ontario—*Mines, Bureau of.* Report . . . 1904, pt. 1. plates, fold. maps. 25ᶜᵐ. Toronto, Printed and published by L. K. Cameron, printer to the king's most excellent Majesty, 1904.

Svenska (**Kongliga**) **vetenskaps-akademien.** Handlingar. bandet 37, no. 3. Über die obertriadische fauna der Bäreninsel von Johannes Böhm . . . illus., 7 pl. 31½ᶜᵐ. Stockholm, Kungl. boktryckeriet, P. A. Norstedt & söner, 1903.

Victoria—*Mines, Dept. of*—*Geological survey.* . . . Records . . . vol. i, pt. 3. plates (partly fold.) 24½ᶜᵐ. Melbourne, R. S. Brain, government printer, 1904.

West Virginia—*Geological survey.* [Report] . . . v. 1ᵃ, 2. fold. tab. 23ᶜᵐ. [Morgantown, 1903–04]

Wyoming—*Territorial geologist.* Annual report . . . to the governor . . . January, 1890 . . . fold. plates, fold. tab. 23½ᶜᵐ. Cheyenne, the Cheyenne daily leader steam book print, 1890.

21. BIOLOGY.

Bastian, Henry Charlton. Studies in heterogenesis . . . ix, 354, xxxvii p. xix pl. (16 fold.) 26½ᶜᵐ. London, Oxford [etc.] Williams and Norgate, 1903. 4—35082

Bousfield, Edward Collins. Guide to the science of photo-micrography . . . 2d ed. entirely rewritten, and much enl. xiv, 174 p. front., illus., tab. 22½cm. London, J. & A. Churchill, 1892. Agr 5—101

La **Cellule**, recueil de cytologie et d'histologie générale . . . tome xxi, 2. fasc. fold. plates. 29½ᶜᵐ. Lierre, Typ. de J. van In & cⁱᵉ, [etc., etc.] 1904.

Gage, Simon Henry. The microscope. An introduction to microscopic methods and to histology . . . 9th ed. rev., enl. . . . iv, [2], 299 [i. e. 311] p. illus., plates, 24ᶜᵐ. Ithaca, Comstock publishing company, 1904.
Bibliography: p. [282]–288ᵇ.

Jennings, Herbert Spencer. Contributions to the study of the behavior of lower organisms . . . 256 p. illus. 26½ᶜᵐ. Washington, Carnegie institution of Washington, 1904. [Carnegie institution of Washington. Publication no. 16] 4—33378
"Literature cited": p. 253–256.

Linnæus, Carl von. Caroli a Linné . . . Systema naturæ per regna tria naturæ, secundum classes, ordines, genera, species; cum characteribus, differentiis, synonymis, locis . . . ed. 13, aucta, reformata Cura Jo. Frid. Gmelin . . . 3 v. in 10 pts. iii fold pl. 20ᶜᵐ. Lugduni apud J. B. Delamolliere, 1789–96. Agr 5—17
Vol. 1 in 7 pts.; v. 2 in 2 pts.; v. 3 in 1 pt.

Owens college, *Manchester, Eng.* Studies in biology from the biological departments . . . vol. I–IV. illus., plates (partly double, partly col.) 24–25^{cm}. Manchester, J. E. Cornish, 1886–99.
Vol. I–II, title reads: Studies from the biological laboratories.

Vries, Hugo de. Species and varieties, their origin by mutation; lectures delivered at the University of California . . . ed. by Daniel Trembly Mac Dougal . . . xviii, 847 p. 23^{cm}. Chicago, The Open court publishing company; London, K. Paul, Trench, Trübner & co., ltd., 1905. 5—4499

22. BOTANY.

Acloque, Alexandre. . . . Flores régionales de la France. Nord.—Ouest.—Sud-ouest et Pyrénées.—Région méditerranéenne.—Sud-est et Alpes.—Nord-est, Vosges et Alsace.—Centre.—Environs de Paris. [431] p. 18½^{cm}. Paris, J.-B. Baillière et fils, 1904. Agr 5—276
Various paging.
Geographical supplement to his Flore de France, 1894

Avellar Brotero, Felix de. Phytographia Lusitaniæ, seu novarum, rariorum, et aliarum minus cognitarum stirpium, quæ in Lusitania sponte veniunt, ejusdemque floram spectant, descriptiones iconibus illustratæ . . . 2 v. 181 pl. 32^{cm}. Olisipone, ex typographia regia, 1816–27. Agr 5—18

Babington, Charles Cardale. Manual of British botany, containing the flowering plants and ferns arranged according to the natural orders . . . 9th ed. enl. from the author's manuscripts and other sources, ed. by Henry and James Groves. lii, 580 p. 18½^{cm}. London, Gurney & Jackson (successors to Mr. Van Voorst) 1904. Agr 5—279

Baldrati, Isaia. . . . Catalogo illustrativo della Mostra Eritrea . . . 122 p. incl. front., illus. 23½^{cm}. Bologna, Stab. tip. Zamorani e Albertazzi, 1904. Agr 5—120
At head of title: Esposizione romagnola, Ravenna—maggio-giugno 1904.

Barthelat, Gilbert Joseph. . . . Les mucorinées pathogènes et les mucormycoses chez les animaux et chez l'homme . . . 126, [2] p. 24^{cm}. Paris, F. R. de Rudeval, 1903. Agr 5—36
Thèse—Univ. de Paris.
"Bibliographie": p. 123–126.

Berlese, Augusto Napoleone. Fungi moricolæ. Iconografia e descrizione dei funghi parassiti del gelso. . . . 13, [140], 63 p. 71 col. pl. 24½^{cm}. Padova, Tipografia del seminario, 1889. Agr 5—30
Issued in 10 fasc., 1885–89.

Bernardin, Charles. Guide pratique pour la recherche de soixante champignons comestibles choisis parmi les meilleurs et les plus faciles à déterminer avec certitude . . . Avec une préface de Émile Hinzelin. Ouvrage orné de 12 planches coloriées par M. Max Gillard . . . xxvi, 167, [1] p. xii double col. pl. 17½^{cm}. Saint-Dié (Vosges) A. Weick [1903] Agr 5—35

Bocquillon-Limousin, Henri. Manuel des plantes médicinales coloniales et exotiques . . . Introduction par M. Ém. Perrot . . . vii, 314 p. 16½^{cm}. Paris, J.-B. Baillière et fils, 1905. Agr 5—77

Botanische jahrbücher für systematik pflanzengeschichte und pflanzengeographie . . . Generalregister . . . jahrg. I bis xxx (1881 bis 1902) Im auftrage von redaktion und verlag bearb. von L. Diels und J. Mildbraed. 2 p. l., 173, [1] p. 24^{cm}. Leipzig, W. Engelmann, 1904.

British mycological society. . . . Transactions for . . . 1896/97–1903. plates (partly col.) 24–24½^{cm}. Worcester, E. Baylis & son, steam printers [1897]–1904.

Britten, James. A dictionary of English plant-names. By James Britten . . . and Robert Holland. xxviii, 618 p. 22½^{cm}. London; For the English dialect society, Trübner & co., 1886.   Agr 5—281
"Bibliography": p. xxi–xxiii.

Buc'hoz, Pierre Joseph. Histoire universelle du règne végétal, ou Nouveau dictionnaire physique et œconomique de toutes les plantes qui croissent sur la surface du globe . . . Ouvrage orné de 1200 planches . . . dessinées d'après nature, sur les plantes les plus rares du jardin du roi & de celui de Trianon; & d'après la magnifique collection de plantes déposée dans le cabinet des estampes, à la bibliothèque du roi, commencée & exécutée par ordre & sous les yeux de feu Monseigneur le duc d'Orléans, régent du royaume, par Robert & Audriet, &c., & continuée de nos jours par Mademoiselle Basseporte. . . . 12 v. in 4. *and* atlas of 4 v., 1200 pl. 40^{cm}. Paris, Brunet, 1774–78.   Agr 5—29
Vol. 1 pub. by J. P. Costard, fils & compagnie.
Title-pages wanting to V. 2–3, 5–6.
"Catalogue des ouvrages composés par M. Buc'hoz, selon la date des temps où ils ont paru": v. 1, prelim. p. [9]–15.
"Liste des livres employés pour la rédaction de cet ouvrage": V. 1, prelim. p. [16]–20.

Buitenzorg, *Java.* **Jardin botanique.** Verslag omtrent den staat van 's Lands plantentuin te Buitenzorg over het jaar 1903. front., plates (1 fold.) 26½^{cm}. Batavia, Landsdrukkerij, 1904.

Camus, A. Classification des saules d'Europe et monographie des saules de France, par A. et E.-G. Camus. 386 p. 25½^{cm} *and* atlas of 40 pl. 38½^{cm}. Paris, J. Mersch, imprimeur, 1904.   Agr 5—274
"Bibliographie. Morphologie interne": p. 41–43.
"Table alphabétique des ouvrages cités en abrégé dans la bibliographie et la synonymie": p. [372]–377.

[Cavanilles, Antonio José] Géneros y especies de plantas demostradas en las lecciones públicas de año de 1802. 1 p. l., 285–625 p. 22½^{cm}. [Madrid, 1802]

Čelakovský, Ladislav Josef. Prodromus der flora von Böhmen. Enthaltend die beschreibungen und verbreitungsangaben der wildwachsenden und im freien kultivirten gefässpflanzen des königreiches . . . Hrsg. von dem Comité für die naturwissenschaftliche durchforschung Böhmens. 4 pts. in 3 v. fold. pl. 27½^{cm}. Prag, Selbstverlag des Comité's, 1867–81. [Beide comités für die landesdurchforschung, Prag. Archiv für die naturwissenschaftliche landesdurchforschung von Böhmen. Bd. I; II, th. 2; III, abth. 3; IV, no. 3]   Agr 5—19
Pt. 4 pub. by F. Řivnáč.
Paged continuously: 1. th.: 5 p. l., viii, 112 p.; 2. th.: 2 p. l., [113]–388 p.; 3. th.: 2 p. l., 389–691, [8] p.; 4. th.: 4 p. l., [692]–955 p.
CONTENTS.—1. th. Gefässkryptogamen, gymnospermen und monocotylen. 1867.—2. th. Apetale und sympetale dicotylen. 1871–72.—3. th. Eleutheropetale dicotylen. 1874.—4 th. Nachträge bis 1880 nebst schlusswort, verzeichnissen und register. 1881.

Cesati, Vincenzo, *barone.* Stirpes italicæ rariores vel novæ descriptionibus iconibusque illustratæ . . . Accedunt animadversiones in characteres plantarum pariter tabulis adumbratæ. unp. plates, facsims. 61½ x 45½^{cm}. Mediolani, excudebat A. J. F. Pirola, 1840.   Agr 5—20
Half-title and cover-title read: Iconographia stirpium italicarum universa.
Issued in 3 fasc.; fasc. 2 pub. in 1842.

Chicago, University of—*Hull botanical laboratory.* Contributions. VIII, XI–XII, XVI, XXXII. illus., plates. 24^{cm}. Chicago, The University of Chicago press, 1898–1901.
CONTENTS.—VIII. Winter characters of certain sporangia, [by] C. J. Chamberlain.—XI. The effect of aqueous solutions upon the germination of fungus spores, [by] F. L. Stevens.—XII. The life-history of Lemna minor, [by] O. W. Caldwell.—XVI. The compound oosphere of Albugo bliti, [by] F. L. Stevens.—XXXII. Development of the pollen in some Asclepiadaceæ, [by] T. C. Frye.

Cogniaux, Alfred. Dictionnaire iconographique des orchidées; direction & rédaction par A. Cogniaux; dessins & aquarelles par A. Goossens. 7 sér., no. 4, décembre 1904. col. plates. 14½ x 18^{cm}. Bruxelles, Goossens, 1904.

—— Chronique orchidéenne; supplément au Dictionnaire iconographique des orchidées. 19^{cm}. vol. II, n° 4, décembre 1904. Bruxelles, Goossens, 1904.

Conard, Henry S. The waterlilies. A monograph of the genus Nymphaea . . . 1 p. l., xiii, 279 p. illus., 30 pl. (partly col., incl. front.) 31^{cm}. Washington, Carnegie institution, 1905. (*On verso of t.-p.:* Carnegie institution of Washington. Publication no. 4) .
"Bibliography": p. 243-263.

Congrès international de botanique. *1st, Paris,* 1900. Actes du 1er Congrès international de botanique tenu à Paris à l'occasion de l'Exposition universelle de 1900 . . . Publié par M. Émile Perrot . . . 2 p. l., xxxii, 571, [1] p. illus., plates (1 double, 1 fold., 2 col.) 25^{cm}. Lons-le-Saunier, Impr. et lithographie L. Declume, 1900. . Agr 5—108

Coultas, Harland. The principles of botany, as exemplified in the cryptogamia. For the use of schools and colleges . . . xi p., 1 l., [15]-94 p. illus. 19½^{cm}. Philadelphia, Lindsay and Blackiston, 1853. Agr 5—109

Coville, Frederick Vernon. Desert botanical laboratory of the Carnegie institution, by Frederick Vernon Coville and Daniel Trembly Macdougal. vi, 58 p. illus. (maps, diagr.) xxix pl. (incl. front.) 25½^{cm}. Washington, The Carnegie institution, 1903. [Carnegie institution of Washington. Publication no. 6] 4—19091
"Bibliography. By William Austin Cannon": p. 46-58.

Czapek, Friedrich. Biochemie der pflanzen . . 1. bd. 25½^{cm}. Jena, G. Fischer, 1905.

Detmer, Wilhelm. Beiträge zur theorie des wurzeldrucks . . . 65, [1] p. pl. 22½^{cm}. Jena, H. Dufft, 1877. [*On cover:* Sammlung physiologischer abhandlungen hrsg. von W. Preyer. 1. reihe, 8. hft.] ' Agr 5—110

Druce, George Claridge. The flora of Berkshire; being a topographical and historical account of the flowering plants and ferns found in the county, with short biographical notices of the botanists who have contributed to Berkshire botany during the last three centuries . . . cxcix, [1], 644 p. fold. map in pocket. 20^{cm}. Oxford, The Clarendon press, 1897. Agr 5—275
"List of books and mss. quoted in the Flora": p. cxcii-cxcvii..

Dupetit-Thouars, Louis Marie Aubert Aubert. Histoire particulière des plantes orchidées recueillies sur les trois iles australes d'Afrique, de France, de Bourbon et de Madagascar; par le chevalier Aubert-Aubert du Petit-Thouars . . . Composée de quatre-vingt-onze espèces figurées sur le vivant, et mises à l'eau-forte par l'auteur; rangées méthodiquement et dénommées par deux tableaux synoptiques; enfin décrites de manière à faire connoître tout ce qu'elles présentent de remarquable. vii, [1], 32 p. 110 col. pl., 2 fold. tab. 24½^{cm}. Paris, L'auteur [etc.] 1822. Agr 5—21
Half-title reads: Flore des iles australes d'Afrique. Famille des orchidées.
"Stated in advertisements on the half-title of the author's 'Essais' (1809) to have been begun in 1804."—Catalogue of the books . . . British museum (Natural history)

Faupin, E. . . . Les champignons comestibles et vénéneux. Méthode pratique pour reconnaître les espèces dangereuses et les distinguer des espèces alimentaires les plus communes. 174, [2] p. illus., xi col. pl. 19½^{cm}. Paris, F. Nathan [1903] (Bibliothèque de vulgarisation scientifique) Agr 5—34

Faupin, E. Tableau synoptique des principaux champignons vénéneux comparés aux espèces comestibles avec lesquelles on pourrait les confondre . . . chart of 80 x 60^{cm}. Paris, F. Nathan [1903]

Fedchenko, Aleksieĭ Pavlovich. . . . Puteshestvie v Turkestan . . . tom III. Botanicheskiia izsliedovaniia . . . 3 v. in 1. 30½ᶜᵐ. S.-Peterburg, Moskva, 1876–82.

Agr 5—89

Goebel, Karl Eberhard. Pflanzenbiologische schilderungen. 1. t. illus., IX pl. 24½ᶜᵐ. Marburg, N. G. Elwert'sche verlagsbuchhandlung, 1889.   4—10109

Guéguen, Fernand. . . . Les champignons parasites de l'homme & des animaux. Généralités, classification, biologie, technique.—Clefs analytiques, synonymie, diagnoses, histoire parasitologique, bibliographie. Préface de M. Maxime Radais . . . xvii, 299 p. incl. XII pl. 25ᶜᵐ. Paris, A. Joanin et cie, 1904.   Agr 5—308

Bibliographies interspersed.

Hayne, Friedrich Gottlob. Getreue darstellung und beschreibung der in der arzneykunde gebräuchlichen gewächse, wie auch solcher, welche mit ihnen verwechselt werden können . . . 14 v. front. (v. 12, port.) 648 col. pl. 28½ᶜᵐ. (v. 13, 30ᶜᵐ). Berlin, Auf kosten des verfassers, 1805-[46]   Agr 5—312

Vol. 12 by F. G. Hayne, J. F. Brandt, and J. T. C. Ratzeburg; v. 13 by J. F. Brandt and J. T. C. Ratzeburg; v. 14 by J. F. Klotzsch.

Hoffman, Hermann i. e. Heinrich Carl Hermann. Index fungorum, sistens icones et specimina sicca nuperis temporibus edita; adjectis synonymis . . . Indicis mycologici editio aucta. vi, 153, [1] p. 25ᶜᵐ. Lipsiae, sumptibus A. Förstneri (A. Felix) 1863.   Agr 5—282

Huth, Ernst. . . . Clavis Riviniana, schlüssel zu den kupferwerken des A. Q. Rivinus . . . 1 p. l., 28 p. 26ᶜᵐ. Frankfurt a. O., Königliche hofbuchdruckerei Trowitzsch u. sohn, 1891.

From Jahresbericht über die Oberschule (Realgymnasium) zu Frankfurt an der Oder . . . 1891. Progr. nr. 104.

India—*Botanical survey.* Records of the Botanical survey of India . . . vol. IV, no. 1. An epitome of the British Indian species of Impatiens. By Sir. J. D. Hooker . . . pt. 1. 24½ᶜᵐ. Calcutta, Printed for the government of India at the Government central printing office, 1904.

International catalogue of scientific literature, 2d annual issue. M. Botany. 21½ᶜᵐ. London, Published for the International council by the Royal society of London, 1904.

Kaĭgorodov, Dimitriĭ. Sobiratel gribov . . . Izdanie 4-e, vnov prosmotriennoe . . . viii, 100 p. XIV col. pl. (1 double). 19½ᶜᵐ. S. Peterburg, Izdanie A. S. Suvorina, 1903.   Agr 5—112

The mushroom collector.

Kaempfer, Engelbert. Icones selectæ plantarum, quas in Japonia collegit et delineavit Engelbertus Kæmpfer; ex archetypis in Museo britannico asservatis. 2 p. l., 3 p. 59 pl. (partly double) 45ᶜᵐ. Londini, 1791.   Agr 5—273

Ed. and pub. by Sir Joseph Banks.

Lindern, Franz Balthasar von. Hortus alsaticus; plantas in Alsatia nobili, inprimis circa Argentinam sponte provenientes, menstruo, quo singulæ florent, ordine designans, annexo charactere, loco natali, ac florum colore, additis aliquibus iconibus, æri ad vivum incisis, ut et aliis ad botanices doctrinam rite addiscendam pertinentibus, in usum botanophilorum excursiones facientium conscriptus . . . 8 p. l., 302, [74] p. XII pl. 18ᶜᵐ. Argentorati, impensis J. Beckii, 1747.   Agr 5—113

Lindern, Franz Balthasar von. Tournefortius alsaticus, cis et trans Rhenanus; sive, Opusculum botanicum ope cujus plantarum species, genera ac differentias, præprimis, circa Argentoratum, locis in vicinis cis & trans Rhenum sponte in montibus, vallibus, sylvis, pratis in & sub aquis nascentes, spatioque menstruo florentes tyro sub excursionibus botanicis facillime dignoscere suæque memoriæ in nominibus imprimendis, ex principiis Tournefortii consulere possit, otio privato conscriptum ac aliquibus tabulis æneis illustratum . . . 8 p. l., 160, [32] p. v pl. 18ᶜᵐ. Argentorati, impensis H. L. Stein, 1728.   Agr 5—114

Macbride, Thomas Huston. A key to the more common species of native and cultivated plants occurring in the northern United States; to accompany Macbride's Lessons in botany. iii, 223–326 p. 17ᶜᵐ. Boston, Allyn & Bacon [°1898] Jan. 26, 99–63

MacDougal, Daniel Trembly. Mutants and hybrids of the Oenotheras . . . By D. T. MacDougal assisted by A. M. **Vail,** G. H. Shull, and J. K. Small. 57 p. front., illus. (incl. diagrs.) plates. 25ᶜᵐ. Washington, The Carnegie institution, 1905. (*On verso of t.-p.:* Carnegie institution of Washington, Publication No. 24. Papers of station for experimental evolution at Cold Spring Harbor, New York, no. 2) "Bibliography": p. 56–57.

Macé, Charles. Étude sur les mycoses expérimentales (aspergillose et saccharomycose) . . . 67, [1] p. illus. 25ᶜᵐ. Paris, F. R. de Rudeval, 1903. Agr 5—32 "Bibliographie" : p. [61]–67.

Mackay, James Townsend. Flora hibernica, comprising the flowering plants, ferns, Characeæ, Musci, Hepaticæ, Lichenes, and Algæ of Ireland, arranged according to the natural system with a synopsis of the genera according to the Linnæan system . . . xxxiv, [3], 279, [1] p. 23ᶜᵐ. Dublin, W. Curray jun. and company; London, Simpkin, Marshall and co.; [etc., etc.] 1836. Agr 5—28

Magnol, Pierre. Petri Magnol . . . Prodromus historiæ generalis plantarum in quo familiæ plantarum per tabulis disponuntur. 15 p. l., 79, [15] p. 17ᶜᵐ. Monspelij, ex typographiâ G. & H. Pech fratrum, 1689. Agr 5—22

Maiden, Joseph Henry. A critical revision of the genus Eucalyptus . . . pt. v. 25–28 pl. 31ᶜᵐ. Sydney, W. A. Gullick, government printer, 1904.

Maly, Karl. Beiträge zur kenntniss der flora Bosniens und der Herzegowina . . . [165]–309 p. 22½ᶜᵐ. [Wien, 1904] Agr 5—278 "Separat-abdruck aus den 'Verhandlungen' der K. K. Zoologisch-botanischen gesellschaft in Wien (jahrg. 1904)"

Michael, Edmund. Führer für pilzfreunde. Die am häufigsten vorkommenden essbaren, verdächtigen und giftigen pilze . . . 2. bd. col. plates. 19½ᶜᵐ. Zwickau, Förster & Borries, 1902.

New South Wales—*Botanic gardens, Director of.* . . . Botanic gardens and domains (report for the year 1903) 33ᶜᵐ. [Sydney, W. A. Gullick, government printer, 1904]

Nooten, *Mme.* Berthe Hoola van. . . . Fleurs, fruits et feuillages choisis de la flore et de la pomone de l'ile de Java . . . 3 p. l., 40 l. 40 col. pl. 60½ᶜᵐ. Bruxelles, E. Tarlier, 1863. Agr 5—307 In French and English. Issued in 10 pts., 1863–64.

Penzig, Otto Albert Julius. Icones fungorum javanicorum, von O. Penzig und P. A. Saccardo. 2 v. lxxx pl. (partly col.) 25½ᶜᵐ. (v. 2. 25ᶜᵐ) Leiden, Buchhandlung und druckerei vormals E. J. Brill, 1904. 4—21889 Text forms revised and enlarged edition of the authors' "Diagnoses fungorum novorum in insula Java collectorum," which appeared in 3 articles in Malpighia, vol. XI, XV, 1897–1902. CONTENTS.—[1] Text.—[2] Tafeln.

Perkins, Janet Russell. Fragmenta floræ Philippinæ. Contributions to the flora of the Philippine Islands . . . fasc. III. pl. 25½ᶜᵐ. Leipzig, Gebrüder Borntraeger; [etc., etc.], 1905.

Pfeffer, Wilhelm. Pflanzenphysiologie. Ein handbuch der lehre vom stoffwechsel und kraftwechsel in der pflanze . . . 2. völlig umgearb. aufl. 2 bd., 2 hälfte. 24ᶜᵐ. Leipzig, W. Engelmann, 1904. Completes the work.

Rattan, Volney. A popular California flora, or, Manual of botany for beginners. Containing descriptions of flowering plants growing in central California, and westward to the ocean. With illustrated introductory lessons, especially adapted to the

Pacific coast. . . . 6th rev. ed. xxviii, 138 p. illus. 20ᶜᵐ. San Francisco, A. L. Bancroft and company, 1885. • Agr 5—116
Paging irregular: 14ᵃ·ᵈ, 20ᵃ—ᵇ, 38ᵃ—ᵇ, and 88ᵃ ᵇ inserted, making a total of 176 pages.

Recueil des travaux botaniques néerlandais publié par la Société botanique néer. landaise . . . no. 2–4. illus., plates (1 fold., 1 col.) 23½ᶜᵐ. Nimègue, F. E. MacDonald, 1904.
Completes vol 1.

Reichenbach, Heinrich Gottlieb Ludwig. Icones floræ Germanicæ et Helveticæ simul terrarum adjacentium ergo mediæ Europæ. Opus auctoribus L. Reichenbach et H. G. Reichenbach fil. conditum, nunc continuatum auctore Dre. G. equite Beck de Mannagetta. Tom: xix, ii, decas 1. Hieracium ii conditum, nunc continuatum, auctore Dr. J. Murr . . . H. Zahn . . . J. Pöll. 8 col. pl. 31½ᶜᵐ. Lipsiæ et Geræ, sumptibus F. de Zezschwitz [1904].

Reneaulme, Paul de. Pavli Renealmi . . . Specimen historiæ plantarum. Plantæ typis æneis expressæ. 3 p. l., 152, [2], 47 p. illus. 23½ᶜᵐ. Parisiis, apud H. Beys, 1611. Agr 5—117

Rosenthaler, L. Grundzüge der chemischen pflanzenuntersuchung . . . 2 p. l., 124 p. 20ᶜᵐ. Berlin, J. Springer, 1904. Agr 5—277
"Literatur": p. [118]-120.

Saccardo, Pier Andrea. . . . La botanica in Italia. Materiali per la storia di questa scienza . . . 2 v. 33 x 24ᶜᵐ. Venezia, Tip. C. Ferrari, 1895–1901. (Memorie, Reale istituto veneto di scienze, lettere ed arti. vol. xxv, no. 4; vol. xxvi, no. 6) 3—23293

Schaffner, John H. . . . Ecological study of Brush Lake, by John H. Schaffner, Otto E. Jennings, and Fredrick J. Tyler . . . 2 p. l., [151]–165 p. front., illus. 23½ᶜᵐ. Columbus, Ohio, Spahr & Glenn, printers, 1904. (Ohio state academy of science. Special papers, no. 10) Agr 5—306
At head of title: Proceedings of the Ohio state academy of science, vol. IV, pt. 4.

Schweinfurth, Georg. Beitrag zur flora aethiopiens . . . 1 abth. xii, 311 p. iv pl. (2 double) 33½ᶜᵐ. Berlin, G. Reimer, 1867. Agr 5—313
No more published.
Bibliography: p. x-xi.

Simonds, Arthur B. Catalogue of the phænogamous and vascular cryptogamous plants of Fitchburg and vicinity. By Arthur B. Simonds, class of '86· Geo. F. Whittemore, class of '86· William G. Farrar, class of '87· E. Adams Hartwell, science teacher. Fitchburg high school. iv, [5]–39 p. 23½ᶜᵐ. Fitchburg, Mass., Fitchburg Agassiz association, 1885. Agr 5—119
Cover-title: Flora of Fitchburg and vicinity.

Società crittogamologica italiana residente in Milano. Atti . . . ser. 2, vol. i-iii. plates. 27ᶜᵐ. Milano, 1878-[84]

Söderbaum, Henrik Gustav. . . . Om nyare metoder att i jordbukets [!] tjänst tillgodogöra luftens kväfve . . . 27 p. 24ᶜᵐ Stockholm, P. A. Norstedt & söner, 1905. (Meddelanden från Kungl. landtbruks-akademiens experimentalfält, n: o 85) Agr 5—299
"Litteraturförteckning:" p. 26–27.
"Aftryck ur Kungl. landtbruks-akademiens handlingar och tidskrift för år 1904."

Spiegel, Adrian. . . . Isagoges in rem herbariam, libri duo. 272, [16] p. 11 x 6ᶜᵐ. Lvgdvni Batavorum, ex officina Elzeviriana, 1633. Agr 5—309
Engr. t.-p.   •

Trautvetter, Ernst Rudolph von. Decas plantarum novarum, auctoribus E. R. a Trautvetter. E. L. Regel. C. J. Maximowicz. K. J. Winkler. 10 p. col. pl. 30½ᶜᵐ. Petropoli, 1882. [With Fedchenko, A. P. . . . Puteshestvie v Turkestan . . . tom iii. Botanicheskiia izsliedovaniia . . . 1876–82. 3 v. in 1] Agr 5—90

Trotter, Alessandro. "Cecidotheca italica;" o, Raccolta di galle italiane determinate preparate ed illustrate. fasc. IX–XII (n. 201–300). 32½ᶜᵐ. Avellino, 1904.

At head of title: Dr. A. Trotter e Dr. G. Cecconi.

Consists of dried specimens, with letterpress descriptions mounted on detached sheets.

Vahl, M. Madeiras vegetation, geografisk monografi. . . . 4 p. l., 172 p., 1 l. fold. map. 23½ᶜᵐ. København og Kristiania, Gyldendalske boghandel, Nordisk forlag, 1904. **Agr 5—284**

"Benyttet litteratur": p. [161]–171.

Inaug.-dis.—Copenhagen.

Volckamer, Johann Georg. Flora noribergensis; sive, Catalogus plantarum in agro noribergensi tam sponte nascentium, quam exoticarum, & in φιλοβοτάνων viridariis, ac medico præcipuè horto aliquot abhinc annis enutritarum, cum denominatione locorum in genere, ubi proveniunt, ac mensium, quibus vigent, florentque; addita singulis exoticis cultura, propagandique ratione, cum generum & specierum, tam summorum, quam infimorum notis characteristicis, ex Morisono, Ammanno, Hermanno, Rajo atque Rivino partim, partim & ex ipso naturæ libro propriis observationibus depromptis . . . 11 p. l., 407, [5] p. plates. 21 x 16½ᶜᵐ. Noribergæ, sumtibus Michaellianus, 1700. **Agr 5—303**

Wagner, Rudolf. Beiträge zur kenntnis der gattung Trochodendron Sieb. et Zucc. . . . [409]–422 p. illus. 28ᶜᵐ. Wien, A. Hölder, 1903.

"Separat-abdruck aus dem XVIII. bd. der Annalen des K. K. Naturhistorischen hofmuseums."

Wehmer, Carl. . . . Die pilzgattung Aspergillus in morphologischer, physiologischer und systematischer beziehung unter besonderer berücksichtigung der mitteleuropæischen species . . . 157 p., 1 l. v pl. (1 col.) 31½ᶜᵐ. Genève, Imprimerie C. Eggimann & cⁱᵉ, 1901. (Mémoires de la Société de physique et d'histoire naturelle de Genève. tome XXXIII (2. ptie.) n° 4) **Agr 5—37**

"Litteratur": p. [5]–15.

Wood, John Medley. Natal plants. v. 5. pt. 1. Grasses . . . 401–425 pl. 27½ᶜᵐ. Durban, Robinson & co., ltd., printers, 1904.

23. ZOOLOGY.

Amsterdam, Koninklijk zoölogisch genootschap "Natura artis magistra" te. Bijdragen tot de dierkunde . . . 17ᵉ en 18ᵉ afl. VIII pl. (1 col.) 36½ᶜᵐ. Leiden, Boekhandel en drukkerij voorheen E. J. Brill, 1893–1904.

California—*Fish commissioners, State board of.* Eighteenth biennial report . . . for the years 1903–04. illus. 23ᶜᵐ. Sacramento, W. W. Shannon, superintendent state printing, 1904.

Cassinia; a bird annual. Proceedings of the Delaware valley ornithological club of Philadelphia. no. 5–8; 1901–04. plates, ports., map, fold. tables. 25½ᶜᵐ. [Philadelphia] 1901–05.

Delaware valley ornithological club of Philadelphia. Abstract of the proceedings . . . for 1890–1900. no. [I]–IV. pl. 23ᶜᵐ. [n. p.] Published by the club, 1892–1901.

Diesing, Karl Moritz. Systema helminthum . . . Sumptibus Academiae Caesareae scientiarum. 2 v. 22½ᶜᵐ. Vindobonae, apud W. Braumüller, 1850–51. **Agr 5—257**

Festschrift zum achtzigsten geburtstage des Herrn geheimen regierungsrats Prof. Dr. Karl Möbius in Berlin. 4 p. l., 654 p. illus., 19 pl. (partly double, partly fold., partly col., incl. maps) port. 24ᶜᵐ. Jena, G. Fischer, 1905. (*Added t.-p.:* Zoologische jahrbücher. Hrsg. von Prof. Dr. J. W. Spengel . . . supplement VIII) **Agr 5—541**

Friderich, C. G. Naturgeschichte der deutschen vögel einschliesslich der sämtlichen vogelarten Europas . . . 5. verm. und verb. aufl., bearb. von Alexander Bau.

lfg. 2–24. illus., plates (partly double, partly col.) 27^{cm}. Stuttgart, Sprösser & Nägele [1904–05]
Completes the work.
"Uebersicht über die einschlägige literatur" in lfg. 22.

Godman, John Davidson. American natural history . . . Part i.—Mastology . . . 3 v. plates. 22^{cm}. Philadelphia, H. C. Carey & I. Lea [etc.] 1826–28.
No more published.   2—7969

Hofer, Bruno. . . . Handbuch der fischkrankheiten . . . 1 p. l., xv, 359 p. illus., xviii col. pl. 23½^{cm}. München, Verlag der Allg. fischerei-zeitung, 1904.
At head of title: Aus der Kgl. Bayer. Biol. Versuchsstation für fischerei.   Agr 5—97

Hutton, Friedrich Wollaston. Index faunæ Zealandiæ . . . Published for the Philosophical institute of Canterbury, New Zealand. viii, 372 p. 22^{cm}. London, Dulau & co., 1904.   Agr 5—98
"Bibliography": p. 21–23.

Italy—*Agricoltura, industria e commercio, Ministero di—Agricoltura, Direzione generale dell'.* . . . Annali di agricoltura 1904. Lavori eseguiti nella R. Stazione di piscicoltura di Roma. plates (partly fold.) 23½^{cm}. Roma, Tipografia nazionale di G. Bertero e c., 1904.

Mayer, Alfred Goldsborough. . . . The Atlantic palolo. . . . illus., col. pl. 25^{cm}. New York, Macmillan company, 1902. (The Museum of the Brooklyn institute of arts and sciences. Science bulletin, vol. 1, no. 3)

Millais, John Guille. The mammals of Great Britain and Ireland . . . vol. i. front., plates (partly col.). 36 x 32^{cm}. London, New York and Bombay, Longmans, Green and co., 1904.

New Jersey state museum. Annual report . . . 1901, 1903. fronts. (1 fold. map), plates (partly col.) 23^{cm}. Camden, 1902–04.
Report for 1903 includes a list of the birds of New Jersey, with a description of each, and illustrations, and the law protecting birds, &c., 1903.

Rörig, Adolf. Das wachstum des schädels von Capreolus vulgaris, Cervus elaphus und Dama vulgaris. Von Adolf Rörig . . . viii, 320 p., 4 l. illus., iv pl. 31½^{cm}. Stuttgart, E. Nägele, 1904. (*Added t.-p.:* Bibliotheca medica . . . abt. 4. Anatomie. Hrsg. von Professor Dr. Wilh. Roux. A. hft. 4)   Agr 5—253

Rosenhauer, Wilhelm Gottlob. Die thiere Andalusiens nach dem resultate einer reise zusammengestellt, nebst den beschreibungen von 249 neuen oder bis jetzt noch unbeschriebenen gattungen und arten . . . viii, 429 p. iii pl. incl. front. 23^{cm}. Erlangen, T. Blaesing, 1856.   Agr 5—100

Schubert, Ottokar. Die Radbusa und ihre nebenläufe mit besonderer berücksichtigung der fischerei-verhältnisse. Ein versuch zur nachahmung für die beschreibung der fischgewässer in Deutschböhmen. Mit einem vorworte von Prof. Howorka-Kadden. Anhang: Beschreibung einiger grenzbäche (Donaugebiet) . . . 96 p. fold. map. 26^{cm}. Prag, Verlag der Deutschen sektion des Landeskulturrates für das königreich Böhmen, 1903. (*On cover:* Arbeiten der Deutschen sektion des Landeskulturrates für das königreich Böhmen. hft. vi)   Agr 5—125

Société royale zoologique et malacologique de Belgique. Annales . . . t. xxxviii; année 1903. illus. 25½^{cm}. Bruxelles, P. Weissenbruch, Impr. du roi, 1904.

Strubell, Adolf Wilhelm. Untersuchungen über den bau und die entwicklung des rübennematoden Heterodera schachtii Schmdt. . . . 49, [3] p. ii double pl. (1 col.) 31½^{cm}. Cassel, T. Fischer, 1888. (*Added t.-p.:* Bibliotheca zoologica. Original-abhandlungen aus dem gesammtgebiete der zoologie. Hrsg. von Dr. Rud. Leuckart und Dr. Carl Chun . . . hft. 2)
"Litteratur-verzeichniss": Verso p. 49.

Trouessart, Édouard Louis. Catalogus mammalium tam viventium quam fossilium . . . Quinquennale supplementum, anno 1904, fasc. III. Tillodontia, Ungulata et Sirenia. 24½ᶜᵐ. Berolini, R. Friedländer & sohn, 1905.

Wheelock, *Mrs.* Irene Grosvenor. Nestlings of forest and marsh . . . 257 p., 1 l. front., illus., plates. 19½ᶜᵐ. Chicago, A. C. McClurg & co., 1902.   2—10845

Wiegmann, Arend Friedrich August. A. F. A. Wiegmann's und J. F. Ruthe's Handbuch der zoologie. 3. aufl. Umgearb., verm. und verb. von Dr. Franz Herrmann Troschel und Johann Friedrich Ruthe. iv, 651, [1] p. 21ᶜᵐ. Berlin, C. G. Lüderitz, 1848.   Agr 5—254

Der **Zoologische** garten (zoologischer beobachter) zeitschrift für beobachtung, pflege und zucht der tiere. Organ der zoologischen gärten Deutschlands, hrsg. von der "Neuen zoologischen gesellschaft" in Frankfurt a. M. . . . I.–XVII., XXI.–XXV., XXVII.–XXXVII. jahrg. illus., plates. 23½ᶜᵐ. Frankfurt a. M., Mahlau & Waldschmidt [etc.] 1860–96.
Minor changes in title.

24. HUNTING.

The **American** shooter's manual, comprising such plain and simple rules as are necessary to introduce the inexperienced into a full knowledge of all that relates to the dog, and the correct use of the gun; also a description of the game of this country, by a gentleman of Philadelphia county. [v]–xii, [13]–249, [2] p. front., plates. 18ᶜᵐ. Philadelphia, Carey, Lea & Carey, 1827.   Agr 5—16

Connecticut—*Fisheries and game, State commissioners of.* . . . Fifth biennial report . . . for the years 1903–1904 . . . plates. 23½ᶜᵐ. Hartford, Press of the Hartford printing co., 1904.

Forest and stream publishing co. Big game and fish map of the province of New Brunswick . . . comp. & drawn by T. G. Loggie. 76½ x 61ᶜᵐ. New York, 1899.

Hanbury, David T. Sport and travel in the northland of Canada . . . xxxii, 319 p. col. front., plates (partly col.) fold. maps. 23ᶜᵐ. London, E. Arnold, 1904.
    Agr 5—96

Macintyre, Donald. Hindu-Koh: Wanderings and wild sport on and beyond the Himalayas, by Major-General Donald Macintyre . . . New ed. xviii, 362 p. front., illus., plates. 21ᶜᵐ. Edinburgh and London, Blackwood and sons, 1891.   Agr 5—332

Maine—*Inland fisheries and game, Commissioners of.* Report . . . for the year 1904. front., illus., plates. 23ᶜᵐ. Augusta, Kennebec journal print, 1905.

The **National** sportsman; an illustrated monthly magazine devoted to sport with rod, dog, rifle, and gun [May, 1902–June, 1904; v. 9–12, no. 8]. illus., plates. 24½ᶜᵐ. Boston, The Tilton publishing company [1092–04].

25. ENTOMOLOGY.

Banks, Nathan. Some *Arachnida* from California . . . 1 p. l., 331–376 p. pl. XXXVIII–XLI. 25ᶜᵐ. San Francisco, The Academy, 1904. (Proceedings of the California academy of sciences. Third series. Zoology. vol. III, no. 13)   5—1828

Bechstein, Johann Matthäus. Vollständige naturgeschichte der schädlichen forstinsekten. Ein handbuch für forstmänner, cameralisten und oekonomen. Hrsg. von Johann Matthäus Bechstein . . . und Georg Ludwig Scharfenberg . . . 3 v. XIII col. pl. 23¼ x 19½ᶜᵐ. Leipzig, C. F. E. Richter, 1804–05.   Agr 5—249

Bericht über die wissenschaftlichen leistungen im gebiete der entomologie während des jahres 1900, 1902. 24½ᶜᵐ. Berlin, Nicolaische verlags-buchhandlung, 1901–03. (*On cover:* Archiv für naturgeschichte . . . 67. jahrg., II. bd., 2. hft., 2. hälfte, 1. lfg.; 69. jahrg., II. bd., 2. hft., 1. lfg.)

Blanchon, H. L. Alphonse.   . . . Manuel pratique du sériculteur.   . . . 144 p.
18½ᶜᵐ. Paris, C. Amat, 1905.   ,   Agr 5—290

Carpenter, George Herbert.   . . . Injurious insects and other animals observed
in Ireland during the year 1903.   . . . 2 pl. 21½ᶜᵐ. [Dublin] 1904. (The economic
proceedings of the Royal Dublin society. vol. I., pt v., no. 12.)

Caudell, Andrew Nelson . . . Orthoptera from southwestern Texas. Collected
by the museum expeditions of 1903, 1904 . . . 1 p. l., 105–116 p. VI–VII pl.
25½ᶜᵐ. New York, pub. by the Macmillan company for the Brooklyn institute of
arts and sciences, 1904. (The museum of the Brooklyn institute of arts and sciences.
Science bulletin, vol. 1, no. 4)

Dahlbom, Anders Gustav. Exercitationes hymenopterologicæ . . . ad illus-
trandam faunam svecicam . . . 6 pts. in 1 v. 19ᶜᵐ. Londini Gothorum, typis
Berlingianis, 1831–33.   Agr 5—512
Inaug.-dis.—Lund.

Distant, William Lucas. Insecta transvaaliensia: a contribution to a knowledge
of the entomology of South Africa . . . pt. VI. illus., XIII–XV pl. 32½ᶜᵐ. London,
West, Newman & co. [1904]

Duftschmid, Kaspar. Fauna Austriæ, oder Beschreibung der österreichischen
insecten für angehende freunde der entomologie . . . 3 v. 19ᶜᵐ. Linz und Leipzig, Im verlag der K. K. Priv. Akademischen kunst-, musik-, und buchhandlung,
1805–25.   Agr 5—144

Enteman, Wilhelmine Marie. Coloration in Polistes . . . 88 p. illus., VI col.
pl. (partly fold.) 25½ᶜᵐ. Washington, The Carnegie institution, 1904. (On verso of
t.-p.: Carnegie institution of Washington. Publication no. 19)   5—4160
Bibliography: p. 87–88.

Fabre, Jean Henri Casimir. . . . Souvenirs entomologiques (7.-8. sér.) Études
sur l'instinct et les mœurs des insectes. illus. 23ᶜᵐ. Paris, C. Delagrave [1900–03]

Geer, Carl de. Caroli lib. bar. de Geer . . . Genera et species insectorvm e
generosissimi avctoris scriptis extraxit, digessit, latine qvoad partem reddidit, et
terminologiam insectorvm Linneanam addidit Anders Iahan Retzivs . . . 2 p. l.,
vi, [7]–220, 32. 19½ᶜᵐ. Lipsiae, apvd S. L. Crvsivm, 1783.   Agr 5—152

Grimshaw, Percy Hall. . . . Diptera Scotica: IV.—Orkney and Shetland . . .
22ᶜᵐ. [n. p., 1905]
Reprinted from "The Annals of Scottish natural history," January, 1905.

Harris, Thaddeus William. A treatise on some of the insects of New England
which are injurious to vegetation . . . 2 p. l., 459 p. 24½ᶜᵐ. Cambridge, J. Owen,
1842.   Agr 5—58

Henschel, Gustav A. O. Die schädlichen forst- und obstbaum-insekten, ihre
lebensweise und bekämpfung. Praktisches handbuch für forstwirthe und gärtner
. . . 3. neubearb. aufl. xii, 758 p. illus. 22½ᶜᵐ. Berlin, P. Parey, 1895. Agr 5—155

Hine, James Stewart. . . . Tabanidae of the western United States and Canada . . . [217]–248 p. 23½ᶜᵐ. Columbus, Published by the University, 1904.
(. . . Ohio state university. Contributions from the Department of zoology and
entomology. no. 21)
Reprinted from Ohio naturalist, vol. V, pages 217-249, December, 1904.

Hudson, George Vernon. New Zealand Neuroptera. A popular introduction to
the life-histories and habits of may-flies, dragon-flies, caddis-flies and allied insects
inhabiting New Zealand, including notes on their relation to angling . . . viii p.,
1 l., 102 p., 12 l. XI col. pl. 22½ᶜᵐ. London, West, Newman & co., 1904. Agr 5—158

Jakobson, Georg Georg. Priamokrylyia i lozhnosietchatokrylyia Rossiĭskoĭ
Imperii i sopredielʹnykh stran. Sostavleno G. G. Jakobsonom i V. L. Bianki . . .

po Dr. R. Tümpel'iu Die geradflügler Mitteleuropas . ._. vuipsk vii. 28^{cm}. S.-
Peterburg, Izdanie A. F. Devriena, 1905.

Orthoptera and Pseudoneuroptera of the Russian empire and adjacent countries. By G. G. Jakobson and V. L. Bianchi . . . after Dr. R. Tümpel's Die geradflügler Mitteleuropas.
Completes the work.

Kerremans, Charles. . . . Monographie des buprestides. tome i, 1.-5. livraison.
col. plates. 26^{cm}. Bruxelles, Impr. J. Janssens, 1904-05.

Labram, J. David. Insekten der Schweiz, die vorzüglichsten gattungen je durch
eine art bildlich dargestellt von J. D. Labram. Nach anleitung und text von Dr. ;
Ludwig Imhoff . . . 5 v. in 6. col. plates. 17½^{cm}. Basel, Bei den verfassern,
1836-[45]   Agr 5—289
Issued in 100 pts., 1835-45 (?)

Minnesota—*Entomologist.* Ninth annual report . . . for the year 1904. Third
annual report of F. L. Washburn. illus., col. pl. 22½^{cm}. St. Anthony Park, Agricultural experiment station, 1904.

Morse, Albert Pitts. Researches on North American Acridiidæ . . . 55 p.
illus., 8.pl. incl. front. 26^{cm}. Washington, The Carnegie institution, 1904. [Car-
negie institution of Washington. Publication no. 18]   Agr 5—172

Nees von Esenbeck, Christian Gottfried. Hymenopterorum Ichneumonibus
affinium monographiæ, genera Europæa et species illustrantes . . . 2 v. 21½^{cm}.
Stuttgartiæ et Tubingæ, sumptibus J. G. Cottæ, 1834.   Agr 5—149

New Jersey—*Agricultural college experiment station.* Report on the mosquito
investigations [by John B. Smith] [509]-593 p. illus., plates (1 fold.) fold. plans.
22½^{cm}. [Trenton] 1902.
"Literature cited": p. 593.
From the 23d annual report of the New Jersey state agricultural college experiment station. 1902.

New Jersey—*Agricultural experiment station.* Report . . . upon the mosquitoes
occurring within the state; their habits, life history, &c. Prepared by John
B. Smith . . . v, 482 p. illus., plates (1 fold.) fold. plans. 23^{cm}. Trenton,
MacCrellish & Quigley, state printers, 1904.   Agr 5—291

Nooten, Mme. Berthe Hoola van. Phyllium pulcherrifolium. [2] p. 1 col. pl.
60½^{cm}. [Batavia, 1862]
In Dutch, French, and English.

Padua. R. Stazione bacologica di Padova. Annuario . . . vol. xxxii. illus.,
pl. 24^{cm}. Padova, Tipografia dei Fratelli Gallina, 1904.

Palisot de Beauvois, Ambroise Marie François Joseph. Insectes recueillis en
Afrique et en Amérique, dans les royaumes d'Oware et de Benin, à Saint-Domingue
et dans les Etats-Unis, pendant les années 1786-1797 . . . 2 p. l., xvi, 276 p. col.
plates. 39^{cm}. Paris, Impr. de Fain et compagnie [etc.] 1905.   Agr 5—221
Date of publication given by Hagen and others as 1805-21.

Pictet, A. Édouard. Synopsis des névroptères d'Espagne . . . 2 p. l., 123 p.
14 col. pl. 27½^{cm}. Genève, H. Georg; [etc., etc.] 1865.   Agr 5—226
"Auteurs cités dans cet ouvrage": p. 7-8.

Rebel, Hans. Studien über die lepidopterenfauna der Balkanländer . . . i. t.
Bulgarien und Ostrumelien . . . col. pl. 28^{cm}. [Wien, A. Hölder, 1903]
Separat-abdruck aus dem xviii. bd. der Annalen des K. K. Naturhistorischen hofmuseums.

Romanoff, *grossfürst* Nikolai Michailowitsch, *ed.* Mémoires sur les lépidoptères
. . . tome viii-ix. col. plates. 31-31½^{cm}. Saint-Pétersbourg, 1897-1901.

Rörig, Georg Friedrich Carl. Leitfaden für das studium der insekten und entomo-
logische unterrichtstafeln . . . 2 p. l., 43, [1] p. viii pl. 24^{cm}. Berlin, R. Friedländer & sohn, 1894.   Agr 5—234

Sahlberg, Reinhold Ferdinand. Monographia Geocorisarum Fenniæ . . . 1 p. l., xl, 154 p., 1 l. . 18ᶜᵐ. Helsingforsiæ, ex officina typographica Frenckelliana, 1848.
Inaug.-dis.—Helsingfors. Agr 5—236
Carl Axel von Pfaler, respondent.

Schellenberg, Johann Rudolf. Das geschlecht der land- und wasserwanzen. Nach familien geordnet mit abbildungen . . . 32 p. xiv col. pl. 22½ᶜᵐ. Zürich, Orell, Füssli und compagnie, 1800. Agr 5—238

Stoll, Caspar. Natuurlijke en naar het leven nauwkeurig gekleurde afbeeldingen en beschrijvingen der spoken, wandelende, bladen, zabel-springhanen, krekels, trek-springhanen en kakkerlakken. In alle vier deelen der wereld, Europa, Asia, Afrika en Amerika, huishoudende. Bij een verzameld en beschreven door Caspar Stoll. Représentation exactement colorée d'après nature des spectres ou phasmes, des mantes, des sauterelles, des grillons, des criquets et des blattes. Qui se trouvent dans les quatre parties du monde. L'Europe, l'Asie, l'Afrique et l'Amérique; rassemblées et décrites par Caspar Stoll. 2 v. 70 col. pl. 31ᶜᵐ. Amsterdam, J. C. Sepp et fils, 1813. Agr 5—250
Each vol. has added engr. t.-p. in colors.
Dutch and French in parallel columns.

Thomson, Carl Gustaf. Skandinaviens Coleoptera, synoptiskt bearbetade . . . 10 v. 22ᶜᵐ. Lund, Tryckt uti Lundbergska boktryckeriet, 1859–68. Agr 5—261
Vol. 7 issued in 2 pts.
Vol. 1–3 "Tryckt uti Berlingska boktryckeriet."

Willem, Victor. Recherches sur les collemboles et les thysanoures . . . 144 p. illus., xvii pl. 29ᶜᵐ. Agr 5—247
From Mémoires couronnés et mémoires des savants étrangers de l'Académie royale des sciences, des lettres et des beaux arts de Belgique. v. 58, 1899.

Wollaston, Thomas Vernon. Insecta maderensia; being an account of the insects of the islands of the Madeiran group . . . xliii, 634 p. xiii col. pl. 32½ᶜᵐ. London, J. Van Voorst, 1854. Agr 5—248

26. LEGISLATION AND LAW.

. . . The **Federal** reporter, v. 132. Cases argued and determined in the circuit courts of appeals and circuit and district courts of the United States. Permanent ed. October–December, 1904 . . . 22½ᶜᵐ. St. Paul, West publishing co., 1905.

General digest, American and English, annotated; embracing all matter digested in the June, August, and October, 1904, bimonthly advance sheets. Refers to all reports official and unofficial. vol. xviii, new ser. 26ᶜᵐ. Rochester, N. Y., The Lawyers' cooperative publishing company, 1905.

Gould, John Melville. Second supplement to Notes on the Revised Statutes of the United States and the subsequent legislation of Congress, January 1, 1898–March 1, 1904, by John M. Gould . . . and George F. Tucker . . . xiv, 738 p. 29½ᶜᵐ. Boston, Little and company, 1904. 4—9217

New South Wales—*Legislative assembly*. . . . The crown lands act of 1884 (48° Victoriæ, no. 18) . . . of 1889 (53° Victoriæ, no. 21) . . . of 1895 (58° Victoriæ, no. 18) [etc.] . . . and the regulations thereunder, including the timber and quarry regulations and the rules of the land appeal court; with the forms employed and a reference map of the colony. 8th ed. 2 p. l., 491 p. fold. map. 24ᶜᵐ. Sydney, W. A. Gullick, government printer, 1898.

New York (*state*)—*Library*. . . . Bulletin . . . legislation 23 . . . 23ᶜᵐ. Albany, New York state education department, 1904.

Newfoundland—*General assembly*. Acts . . . passed in the fourth year of the reign of His Majesty King Edward VII . . . 24ᶜᵐ. St. John's, J. W. Withers, printer to the king's most excellent Majesty, 1904.

North Carolina—*Supreme court.* North Carolina reports, v. 136. Cases argued and determined in the supreme court . . . fall term, 1904. 22½^{cm}. Raleigh, E. M. Uzzell & co., state printers and binders, 1905.

. . . The **Pacific** reporter, v. 1–78, containing all the decisions of the Supreme courts of California, Kansas, Oregon, Washington, Colorado, Montana, Arizona, Nevada, Idaho, Wyoming, Utah, New Mexico, Oklahoma, and court of appeals of Colorado. Permanent ed. Dec. 27, 1883–Jan. 23, 1905. 26^{cm}. (v. 1–20, 22½^{cm}) St. Paul, Webb publishing co., 1884–1905. (National reporter system. State ser.)

The **Pacific** reporter blue label book . . . Table of cases so arranged as to show where any case cited from the reports of Arizona, California, Colorado, Idaho, Kansas, Montana, Nevada, New Mexico, Oklahoma, Oregon, Utah, Washington, and Wyoming are to be found in the Pacific reporter, covering the reports published from 1883 to April 27, 1903 . . . 2d ed. 26^{cm}. St. Paul, Webb publishing co., 1903.

Vermont—*General assembly.* Acts and resolves passed . . . at the 18th biennial session, 1904 . . . 22^{cm}. Burlington, Free press association, 1904.

27. STATISTICS AND COMMERCE.

Almanaque brasileiro Garnier para o anno de 1903. Publicado sob a direcção de B. F. Ramiz Galvão. anno 1. illus. (incl. ports.) maps. 22½^{cm}. Rio de Janeiro [190–]

Annuario do estado do Rio Grande do Sul para o anno de 1905, publicado sob a direcção de Graciano A. de Azambuja (anno XXI). illus. 18^{cm}. Porto Alegre, Krahe & c^{ia}, succ^{res} de Gundlach & Krahe, 1904.

Arizona—*Governor.* Report . . . for the year ended June 30, 1904. fold. maps. 23^{cm}. Washington, Gov't print. off., 1904.

Austria—*K. K. Ackerbau-ministerium.* Statistisches jahrbuch . . . für 1903. 2. hft. Der bergwerksbetrieb Österreichs im jahre 1903. 2. lfg. Bergwerksverhältnisse (mit ausnahme der bergwerksproduktion und lohnstatistik) naphthastatistik, schlagwetterstatistik. 23^{cm}. Wien, Druck und verlag der K. K. Hof-und staatsdruckerei, 1904.

Baltimore—*Trade, Board of.* Report of the president and directors . . . for the year ending September 30, 1904 . . . 23^{cm}. Baltimore, Fleet-McGinley co., 1904.

Belgium—*Agriculture, Ministère de l'.* . . . Recensement agricole de 1903 . . . 27½^{cm}. Bruxelles, 1904.
At head of title: Statistique de la Belgique.

Belgium—*Agriculture et des travaux publics, Ministère de l'.* Statistique de la Belgique. Agriculture. Recensement général de 1895 . . . Partie documentaire . . . t. IV. 26½^{cm}. Bruxelles [Impr. E. Daem] 1899.   3—15764
Completes work.
CONTENTS.—Répartition des bois et des terrains incultes. Produits des propriétés boisées (moyenne des années 1892-1893-1894)

——— — . . . Partie analytique. 2 p. l., viii, 552 p. 27½^{cm}. Bruxelles [Impr. E. Daem] 1900.   3—15765

Berlin—*Statistisches amt.* Berliner statistik . . . 3. hft. Lohnermittelungen und haushaltrechnungen der minder bemittelten bevölkerung im jahre 1903. pl. 29^{cm}. Berlin, Druck und verlag P. Stankiewicz' buchdruckerei, 1904.

Boston—*Statistical dept.* . . . Special publications no. 10. Receipts and expenditures of ordinary revenue 1899–1903. fold. tab. 30^{cm}. Boston, Municipal printing office, 1904.

California—*Controller.* . . . Biennial report . . . for the 54th fiscal year, ending June 30, 1903, and the 55th fiscal year, ending June 30, 1904. fold. tables. 23½^{cm}. Sacramento, W. W. Shannon, superintendent state printing, 1905.

California—*Labor statistics, Bureau of.* Eleventh biennial report . . . 1904. 23½ᶜᵐ. Sacramento, W. W. Shannon, superintendent state printing, 1904.

Canada—*Census office.* Fourth census of Canada, 1901. vol. ii. Natural products. 25ᶜᵐ. Ottawa, S. E. Dawson, printer to the king's most excellent Majesty, 1904.

Canada—*Customs dept.* . . . Tables of the trade and navigation of the Dominion of Canada for . . . 1901/02–1903/04, compiled from official returns . . . tables. 25ᶜᵐ. Ottawa, Printed by S. E. Dawson, printer to the king's most excellent Majesty, 1902–04.

Canada—*Inland revenues, Dept. of.* . . . Report, returns and statistics . . . for the fiscal year ended June 30, 1904 . . . 24½ᶜᵐ. Ottawa, Printed by S. E. Dawson, printer to the king's most excellent Majesty, 1904.
CONTENTS.—pt. 1. Excise, &c.—pt. 2. Inspection of weights and measures, gas and electric light.

Cape of Good Hope—*Statistical dept.* . . . Report on returns in statistical register, 1903. 33½ᶜᵐ. [n p., n. d.]

Cape of Good Hope—*Statistical dept.* Statistical register . . . for the year 1903, including approximate census population results for 1904, with supplement for half-year, 1904. fold. tab. 33½ᶜᵐ. Cape Town, Cape times, limited, government printers, 1904.

Chile—*Estadística comercial, Oficina de.* . . . Estadística comercial de la República de Chile correspondiente al año de 1903. 34ᶜᵐ. Valparaiso, Impr. del universo de G. Helfmann, 1904.

Connecticut—*Labor statistics, Bureau of.* . . . Twentieth annual report . . . for the year ended November 30, 1904. illus. 22½ᶜᵐ. Meriden, Journal publishing company, 1904.

Denmark—*Statistisk bureau.* . . . Statistisk aarbog. 9. aargang, 1904 . . . tables. 25ᶜᵐ. København, H. H. Thieles bogtrykkeri [1904]
Text in Danish and French.

Denmark—*Statistisk bureau.* . . . Statistisk tabelværk. 5. række, litra A, nr. 4, 5. række, litra D, nr. 14. tables. 29½x24ᶜᵐ. København, B. Lunos bogtrykkeri, 1904.

Denmark—*Statistisk bureau.* . . . Statistiske meddelelser . . . 4. række, 16. bd. tables. 23½ᶜᵐ. København, B. Lunos bogtrykkeri, 1904.

Finland—*Government.* . . . Finlands handel på Ryssland och utrikes orter samt uppbörden vid tullverket år 1903. diagr. 26ᶜᵐ. Helsingfors, Kejserliga senatens tryckeri, 1904. (Bidrag till Finlands officiella statistik i A:23)

France—*Douanes, Direction générale de.* . . . Tableau général du commerce et de la navigation, année 1903. 1. v. Commerce de la France avec ses colonies et les puissances étrangères. 36ᶜᵐ. Paris, Imprimerie nationale, 1904.

Germany—*Kaiserliches statistisches amt.* Statistik des Deutschen Reichs . . . bd. 159. 32ᶜᵐ. Berlin, Puttkamer & Mühlbrecht, 1904.
CONTENTS.—Auswärtiger handel des deutschen zollgebiets im jahr 1903 . . . 2. teil. Darstellung nach warengattungen.

Gt. Brit.—*Agriculture and fisheries, Board of.* . . . Agricultural returns, 1904. (Produce of crops.) Tables showing the total produce and yield per acre of the principal crops in each county of Great Britain, with summaries for the United Kingdom. 24½ᶜᵐ. London, Printed for H. M. Stationery off., by Wyman and sons, limited, 1905.

Gt. Brit.—*Foreign office.* Reports on the finances, administration, and condition of the Sudan, 1903. 24ᶜᵐ. Khartoum, El Sudan printing press, F. Nimr & co. [1904]

Gt. Brit.—*Trade, Board of.* Statistical abstract for the several British colonies, possessions, and protectorates in each year from 1889 to 1893 . . . 41st no. 24ᶜᵐ. London, Printed for H. M. Stationery off., by Wyman and sons, limited, 1904.

Gt. Brit.—*Trade, Board of.* Statistical tables relating to British possessions and protectorates . . . 1902. pt. xxvii. 33½ᶜᵐ. London, Printed for H. M. Stationery off., by Darling & son, ltd., 1904.

Hamburg, Handelskammer zu. Jahresbericht . . . über das jahr 1904. 23ᶜᵐ. Hamburg, Ackermann & Wulff nachfl., Grosardt & Gowa [1904]

Hawaii—*Governor.* Report . . . 1903–04. fold. map. 23ᶜᵐ. Washington, Gov't print. off., 1903–04.

Howard, Bartels & co., *comp.* Statistical information relating to stocks, cotton, grain, provisions, live stock, seeds. Crops, imports, exports, etc., of principal countries. A publication for ready office reference. tables. 22 x 33ᶜᵐ. Chicago, Howard, Bartels & co., 1905.

Hungary—*Kön. Ungar. statistisches central-amt.* Publications statistiques hongroises. nouv. sér., 8. v. Commerce extérieur des pays de la couroune hongroise en 1903 . . . 27ᶜᵐ. Budapest, Imprimerie de la Société anonyme athenaeum, 1904.

India—*Bengal*—*Land records and agriculture, Dept. of.* Agricultural statistics of the lower provinces of Bengal for 1903–04. 33ᶜᵐ. Calcutta, Bengal secretariat press, 1904.

India—*Statistical dept.* . . . Agricultural statistics of India for the years 1898–99 to 1902–03. 19th issue, vol. i–ii. 33½ᶜᵐ. Calcutta, Office of the superintendent of government printing, 1904.
    CONTENTS.—I. British India.—II. Native states.

India—*Statistical dept.* . . . Annual statement of the sea-borne trade and navigation of British India with the British Empire and foreign countries in the year ending March 31, 1904, and the four preceding years . . . vol. i (abstract and detailed tables of imports and exports). 35ᶜᵐ. Calcutta, Office of the superintendent of government printing, India, 1904.

India—*Statistical dept.* Area and yield of certain principal crops in India, rice, wheat, cotton, oilseeds, jute, indigo, sugarcane, for various periods from 1891–92 to 1903–04. 34ᶜᵐ. Calcutta, Office of the superintendent of government printing, 1904.

India—*United Provinces of Agra and Oudh*—*Land records and agriculture, Dept. of.* Annual report on the inland trade . . . for the year ending 31st March, 1904. 32½ᶜᵐ. Allahabad, Printed at the United Provinces government press, 1904.

Ireland—*Agriculture and technical instruction, Dept. of.* . . . Agricultural statistics, Ireland, 1904. Report and tables relating to Irish migratory agricultural and other labourers . . . 24½ᶜᵐ. Dublin, Printed for H. M. Stationery off., by A. Thom & co. (limited) 1904.

Ireland—*Agriculture and technical instruction, Dept. of.* . . . Agricultural statistics, Ireland, 1904. Tables showing the extent in statute acres and the produce of the crops for the year 1904. With tables showing the average yearly extent under the principal crops, and the average produce thereof in the ten years 1894–1903; also beekeeping statistics for the season 1903. 24½ᶜᵐ. Dublin, Printed for H. M. Stationery off., by A. Thom & co. (limited) 1905.

Italy—*Agricoltura, industria e commercio, Ministero di*—*Statistica, Direzione generale della.* . . . Statistica della emigrazione italiana per l'estero negli anni 1902 e 1903, e notizie sull' emigrazione da alcuni altri stati. 26ᶜᵐ. Roma, Tipografia nazionale di G. Bertero e c., 1904.

Japan—*Statistique générale, Section de la.* [Annuaire statistique de l'empire du Japon, 1903.] v. 23. 25½ᶜᵐ. [Tokio, 1904.]
    In Japanese.

Kansas City stock yards. [Thirty-fourth annual report of] receipts and shipments of live stock . . . for the year 1904, with a summary of receipts, shipments, and valuation of all kinds of live stock for a term of thirty-four years, ended December 31st, 1904 . . . 18½ᶜᵐ. Kansas City, Tiernan-Dart printing company, 1905.

London—*County council.* . . . Annual report of the proceedings of the council for the year ended 31st March, 1904. 33½ᶜᵐ. [London] J. Truscott & son, ltd., printers [1904]

London—*County council.* Report . . . for the year 1902-3 . . . front. (fold. map) plans (1 fold.) 25ᶜᵐ. London, Printed for the London county council by J. Truscott and son, ltd. [1904]

London—*County council*—*Statistical dept.* Statistical abstract for London, 1904 . . . vol. VII. 24½ᶜᵐ. London, Local government and statistical dept., 1904.

Maine—*Industrial and labor statistics, Bureau of.* Eighteenth annual report . . . 1904. illus. 23ᶜᵐ. Augusta, Kennebec journal print, 1905.

Mecklenburg-Schwerin—*Statistisches bureau.* Beiträge zur statistik Mecklenburgs. . . . 13. bd., 4. hft. tables. 30½ᶜᵐ. Schwerin, Gedruckt in der Bärensprungschen hofbuchdruckerei, 1904.

Mexico—*Fomento, colonización é industria, Secretaría de*—*Estadística, Dirección general de.* . . . Censo general de la república Mexicana verificado el 28 octubre de 1900 . . . 30ᶜᵐ. México, Oficina tip. de la Secretaría de fomento, 1904.
CONTENTS.—Censo y división territorial del estado de Tabasco . . . del estado de Tamaulipas . . . del estado de Nuevo León.

Mexico—*Fomento, colonización é industria, Secretaría de*—*Estadística, Dirección general de.* División territorial de la república Mexicana . . . Estados del Norte. 30ᶜᵐⁱ. México, Oficina tipográfica de la Secretaría de fomento, 1904.

Minnesota—*Auditor of state.* Report . . . for the fiscal years ending July 31, 1903, and July 31, 1904. 23½ᶜᵐ. Minneapolis, The Great western printing co. [1904].

Montana—*Land commissioners, State board of.* First-third, sixth annual report . . . 1891-1892/93, 1896. 23½ᶜᵐ. Helena, State publishing company, 1892-97.

New Jersey—*Statistics of labor and industries, Bureau of.* Twenty-seventh annual report . . . for the year ending October 31st, 1904. plates. 23½ᶜᵐ. Trenton, N. J., MacCrellish & Quigley, state printers, 1904.

New South Wales—*Statistician.* Statistics. Six states of Australia and New Zealand, 1861 to 1903 . . . tables. 21½ᶜᵐ. Sydney, W. A. Gullick, government printer, 1904.

New Zealand—*Registrar-general.* The New Zealand official year-book, 1904, thirteenth year of issue . . . front. (map) col. plates, tables. 21ᶜᵐ. Wellington, J. Mackay, government printer; [etc., etc.] 1904.

Norrgren, L. Russian commercial hand-book; principal points from the Russian law on bills of exchange, on customs formalities in Russian ports, on clearance of goods from the custom house, on stamp duty, on the Russian mining law, and on miscellaneous commercial matters, also comparison of Russian money, weights, and measures with foreign currency and English and French weights and measures . . . XIV, 168 p. 19ᶜᵐ. London, E. Wilson, 1904.   Agr 5—328

North Carolina—*Auditor.* Annual report . . . for the fiscal year ending November 30, 1904. 23½ᶜᵐ. Raleigh, E. M. Uzzell & co., state printers and binders, 1904.

Norway—*Landbrugsdirektpør.* Beretning om høsten i Norge. Aaret 1904 . . . 22½ᶜᵐ. Kristiania, Grøndahl & søns bogtrykkeri, 1904.

Norway—*Statistisk centralbureau.* Statistisk aarbog for kongeriget Norge. 24. aarg. 1904 . . . Annuaire statistique de la Norvége . . . pl. 25ᶜᵐ. Kristiania, H. Aschehoug & co., 1904.

Ontario—*Industries, Bureau of.* Annual report . . . 1903 . . . tables. 25ᶜᵐ. Toronto, Printed by L. K. Cameron, printer to the king's most excellent Majesty, 1904.

Philippine Islands—*Auditor.* Report . . . for the fiscal year ended June 30, 1903. 23ᶜᵐ. Manila, Bureau of public printing, 1903.

Prussia—*Königliches statistisches bureau.* Preussische statistik . . . 187–188 . . . 17 pl. (partly double, partly col.) 33ᶜᵐ. Berlin, Verlag des Königlichen statistischen bureaus, 1904.

Rhode Island—*Industrial statistics, Commissioner of.* Seventeenth annual report . . . made, to the General assembly at its January session, 1904. plates. 23½ᶜᵐ. Providence, E. L. Freeman & sons, state printers, 1904.

Roumania—*Ministerul financelor—Direcţiunea statisticeï generale.* . . . Anuarul statistic al Românieï. Annuaire statistique de la Roumanie. 23ᶜᵐ. Bucuresci, Imprimeria statului, 1904.
In Roumanian and French.

Russia—*Finansov, Ministerstvo.* Rapport . . . pour l'exercice 1905. Budget de l'empire pour l'exercice 1905. 31½ cm. St.-Pétersbourg, Imprimerie de l'Académie impériale des sciences, 1904.

Russia—*Finansov, Ministerstvo—Okladnykh sborov, Departament [Finance, Ministry of—Direct taxes, Dept. of]* . . . Bibliograficheskiï ukazatel zemskoï otsienochno-ekonomicheskoï literatury. pt. 1–5. 29½ᶜᵐ. S.-Peterburg, Tipografiia P. P. Soïkina, 1899–1904.
Bibliographical index of the statistical and economic literature published by zemstvos.
Contents.—pt. I. Moskovskaia guberniia, 1899.—pt. II. Chernigovskaia guberniia, 1899.—pt. III. Tverskaia guberniia, 1900.—pt. IV. Viatskaia guberniia, 1901.—pt. V. Tambovskaia i Riazanskaia gubernii, 1904.

Russia—*Finansov, Ministerstvo—Okladnykh sborov, Departament [Finance, Ministry of—Direct taxes, Dept. of]* Dokhody i raskhody zemstv 34-ᵏʰ guberniï po smietam . . . 1895, 1900. 35½ᶜᵐ. S.-Peterburg, 1896–1901.
Receipts and expenditures of the zemstvos of 34 governments from the estimates.
For 1895 "Dokhody" and "Raskhody" are published separately.

Russia—*Finansov, Ministerstvo—Okladnykh sborov, Departament [Finance, Ministry of—Direct taxes, Dept. of]* Postuplenie kazennykh okladnykh sborov s sel'skikh sosloviï po miesiatsam . . . 1880–1900. 25¼ᶜᵐ. S.-Peterburg, 1903.
Receipts of state direct taxes from the rural classes by months.

Russia—*Finansov, Ministerstvo—Okladnykh sborov, Departament [Finance, Ministry of—Direct taxes, Dept. of]* Svod dannykh o postuplenii kazennykh okladnykh sborov po imperii za desiatilietie 1888–1897 g. g. . . . 28½ᶜᵐ. S.-Peterburg, Tipografiia P. P. Soïkina, 1902.
Summary of data of collection of state direct taxes throughout the empire for the decade 1888–97.

Russia—*Finansov, Ministerstvo—Okladnykh sborov, Departament [Finance, Ministry of—Direct taxes, Dept. of]* . . . Svod sviedieniï o postuplenii i vzimanii kazennykh, zemskikh i obshchéstvennykh okladnykh sborov . . . 1892–99. 36ᶜᵐ. S.-Peterburg, 1902.
Digest of information on receipts and collecting of state, provincial, and local direct taxes.
1892–94 in 2 pts.; 1895–99 in 1 pt.

Russia—*Finansov, Ministerstvo—Zhelieznodorozhnykh diel, Departament [Finance, Ministry of—Railroad affairs, Dept. of]* . . . Khliebnye gruzy . . . 1902. 3 pts. 29ᶜᵐ. S.-Peterburg, 1904. (Svodnaia statistika perevozok po Russkim zhel. dor. no. 37–38) Grain transportation.

San Francisco, Merchants' exchange. Annual statistical report . . . for the year ending June 30, 1904. 23ᶜᵐ. [San Francisco, Commercial publishing company, printers, 1904]

Servia—*Agriculture, de l'industrie et du commerce, Ministère de l'—Statistique, Division de.* . . . Statistique du royaume de la Serbie. tome xxv. 25ᶜᵐ. Belgrade, Imprimerie de l'état du royaume de Serbie, 1904.
Contents.—Statistique agricole du royaume de Serbie pour l'année 1901.

Servia— *Commerce, de l'agriculture et de l'industrie, Ministère du—Statistique, Section du.* . . . Annuaire statistique du royaume de Serbie . . . 6. tome, 1901. 23½ᶜᵐ. Belgrade, Imprimerie de l'état du royaume de Serbie, 1904.

South Australia—*Statistician.* . . . Agricultural and live stock statistics for the year ending March 31st, 1904; with prefatory report. 34ᶜᵐ. Adelaide, C. E. Bristow, government printer, 1904.

South Dakota—*Auditor.* Report . . . for the fiscal year ending June 30, 1904. 23½ᶜᵐ. Aberdeen, News printing co., 1904.

Spain—*Junta consultiva agronómica.* . . . Estadística de la producción de cereales y leguminosas en el año 1903. Resumen de los datos remitidos por los ingenieros del Servicio agronómico regional. 23ᶜᵐ. Madrid, Imprenta de los hijos de M. G. Hernández, 1904.

Styria—*Statistisches landesamt.* Statistische mittheilungen über Steiermark . . . xiv. hft. 26ᶜᵐ. Graz, In kommission bei Leuschner & Lubensky's universitätsbuchhandlung, 1904.
CONTENTS.—Beiträge zur statistik des gemeindehaushaltes. ii. Die schulden der gemeinden mit ende dezember 1901.

Switzerland—*Alkoholverwaltung.* Statistische angaben betreffend die geschäftsführung der eidg. alkoholverwaltung pro 1903. Données statistiques concernant la gestion de la régie fédérale des alcools en 1903. 35½ᶜᵐ. [n. p., 1904]

Switzerland—*Conseil fédéral.* Rapport . . . à l'Assemblée fédérale sur la gestion et le compte de la régie des alcools pour l'année 1903. 21ᶜᵐ. Berne, Impr. C. J. Wyss, 1904.

Switzerland—*Zolldepartement.* Schweizerische handelsstatistik. Jahresbericht 1892. 24ᶜᵐ. Bern, Buchdruckerei J. Schmidt, 1893.

Trans-Mississippi commercial congress. Official proceedings of the 15th session . . . held at St. Louis, Missouri, October 25, 26, 27, and 28, 1904. 23ᶜᵐ. Denver, The Smith-Brooks company, 1904.

Washington (*state*)—*State land commissioners, Board of.* . . . Third biennial report . . . 1898. 23ᶜᵐ. Olympia, G. Hicks, state printer, 1898.

A **Yearbook** and almanac of Newfoundland 1905: containing a calendar and nautical intelligence for the year; authentic and valuable information relating to public offices, institutions, banks, &c., of the colony; together with a carefully revised directory of all towns, villages, and settlements in the island, and the customs tariff (official) corrected to date. 21ᶜᵐ. St. John's, J. W. Withers, King's printer, 1905.

28. ROADS AND ENGINEERING.

Betts, Charles Henry. Highway manual of the state of New York; a complete compilation of all the laws relating to highways, with annotations and forms . . . Official ed. . . . xv, 479 p. 24ᶜᵐ. [Lyons, N. Y.] C. H. Betts, 1904.   4—21094

California—*Highways, Dept. of.* Biennial report . . . December, 1902–04. plates. 23½ᶜᵐ. Sacramento, A. J. Johnston, superintendent state printing, 1902–05.

Egypt—*Public works ministry.* . . . Report upon the administration of the Public works department in Egypt for 1903 . . . fold. map, fold. diagrs. 27½ᶜᵐ. Cairo, National printing dept., 1904.

Hulbert, Archer Butler. Historic highways of America, vol. 15. The future of road-making in America . . . front. (port.) plates. 19½ᶜᵐ. Cleveland, Ohio, The A. H. Clark company, 1905.

North Dakota—*State engineer.* First biennial report . . . 1904 . . . illus., ports. 23ᶜᵐ. Bismarck, Press of the Tribune, 1904.

Sächsische maschinen-prüfungs-station zu Leipzig. . . . Mitteilungen
. .'-: 64–65. illus. 23–23½ᶜᵐ. [Leipzig. 1904]
Sonderabdruck aus der Sächs. landw. zeitschrift nr. 32, 41–42, 1904.

Tóula, Franz. Über wildbach-verheerungen und die mittel, ihnen vorzubeugen
. . . 1 p. l., [501]–622 p. illus. 19ᶜᵐ. [Wien, Im selbstverlage des Vereines zur
verbreitung naturwissenschaftlicher kenntnisse in Wien, 1892] (*On cover:* Schriften
des Vereines zur verbreitung naturwissenschaftlicher kenntnisse in Wien. Nachtrag
zum XXXII. bd., jahrg. 1891/92) Agr 5—329

29. EDUCATION (NOT AGRICULTURAL).

Arkansas—*University, Fayetteville.* Catalogue . . . 30th ed., 1902/03. fronts.
(1 map) 19½ᶜᵐ. Fayetteville [1903]

California polytechnic school, *San Luis Obispo.* First biennial report of the
board of trustees . . . comprising the reports of the director and secretary of the
Board. 1902–04. 22½ᶜᵐ. Sacramento, W. W. Shannon, superintendent state printing, 1905.

Drexel institute of art, science, and industry, *Philadelphia—Library school.*
[Announcement] 1905–06. illus. 21½ᶜᵐ. [Philadelphia, 1905]

Georgia—*State industrial college for colored youths, College, Ga.* Year book . . .
1902–03. 22ᶜᵐ. Athens, The University press, 1903.

Georgia—*University, Athens, Ga.* [General catalogue] . . . for the session 1903–
04. plates (partly fold.) 22½ᶜᵐ. Athens, The University press [1903]

James Millikin university. Catalog . . . [1903/04] illus. 24ᶜᵐ. [Decatur,
Ill., The Review press, 1904] (The James Milliken university bulletin, vol. I, no. 4)

Louisiana—*University and agricultural and mechanical college, Baton Rouge.* Catalogue, 1903/04. front. (fold. plan) 23ᶜᵐ. [Baton Rouge, 1904]

Maine—*Public schools, State superintendent of.* Report . . . for the school year
ending June 30, 1904. pl. 23½ᶜᵐ. Augusta, Kennebec journal print, 1905.

Maine—*University, Orono.* Catalogue . . . 1902/03. front. (fold. plan) 23ᶜᵐ.
Augusta, Kennebec journal print, 1903.

Michigan—*University.* . . . The president's report to the Board of regents for the
academic year ending September 22, 1904. Financial statement for the fiscal year
ending June 30, 1904. 23ᶜᵐ. Ann Arbor, Published by the University, 1904. (University bulletin, new ser., vol. VI, no. I. Nov. 1, 1904)

Pennsylvania—*State college.* Annual report . . . for the year 1902–03. From
July 1, 1902, to June 30, 1903. pt. I—Departments of instruction. pt. II—Agricultu-
ral experiment station. illus., plates, diagrs. (partly double, partly fold.) 24½ᶜᵐ.
[Harrisburg] W. S. Ray, state printer, 1903.

Pennsylvania—*State college.* [Catalogue] . . . 1903/04. 45th year. 20½ᶜᵐ. State
college, 1904.

Tennessee—*Public instruction, Dept. of.* Annual report of the state superintendent
of public instruction . . . for the scholastic year ending June 30, 1904 . . . front.,
plates, ports. 23½ᶜᵐ. Nashville, Foster & Webb, printers and stationers, 1905.

Tuskegee (*Ala.*) **normal and industrial institute.** Twenty-second annual
catalogue . . . 1902/03. front., illus. 21½ᶜᵐ. [Tuskegee, Institute press, 1903]

30. GEOGRAPHY, DESCRIPTION, AND TRAVEL.

Blair, George E., *ed.* The mountain empire Utah; a brief and reasonably authentic
presentation of the material conditions of a state that lies in the heart of the moun-
tains of the West . . . Ed. and pub. by Geo. E. Blair & R. W. Sloan, Salt Lake

City, Utah. 142, [2] p. illus. (incl. ports.) 24^{cm}. [Chicago, Press of W. P. Dunn
co.] ^c1904· 5—4378'
Cover-title: The mountain empire Utah: Bulletin of the plains.

Brazil—*Commissāo representante do Brazil na Louisiana purchase exposiçāo*, 1904..
Brazil at the Louisiana purchase exposition, St. Louis, 1904. 160 p. illus. (incl.
ports.) 25^{cm}. [St. Louis, S. F. Myerson ptg. co., 1904] 5—3931

Japan—*Imperial Japanese commission to the Louisiana purchase exposition.* Japan
in the beginning of the 20th century. 2 p. l., viii, 828 p., 2 l. 23^{cm}. [Tokio, Japan,
Printed at the "Japan times office"] 1904. 4—21898
Ed. by Haruki Yamawaki.

Kurze beschreibung der republik Chile. Nach offiziellen angaben geschrieben.
1 p. l., 80 p. incl. maps. 21½^{cm}. Berlin, Buchdruckerei G. Schenck sohn, 1900.
Agr 5—325

31. GENERAL SERIAL PUBLICATIONS.

American association for the advancement of science. Proceedings . . .
fifty-third meeting held at St. Louis, Mo., Dec., 1903–Jan., 1904. 24½^{cm}. [Wash-
ington] 1904.

American museum of natural history, *New York city.* Bulletin . . . vol. xx;
1904. illus., xiv pl. (1 fold.) 24½^{cm}. New York, Published by order of the trustees,
1904.

American philosophical society. Transactions . . . vol. xxi, new ser., pt. 1.
illus., vii pl. 30^{cm}. Philadelphia, The American philosophical society, 1905.

Amsterdam, Koninklijke akademie van wetenschappen te. Jaarboek . . .
1903. 26½^{cm}. Amsterdam, J. Müller, 1904.

Amsterdam, Koninklijke akadamie van wetenschappen te. . . . Proceed-
ings of the section of sciences. vol. vi. plates (partly fold.) diagrs. 27^{cm}. Amsterdam, J. Müller, 1904.
Issued in 2 pts., 1903–04.

Amsterdam, Koninklijke akademie van wetenschappen te. . . . Ver-
handelingen. (1. sect.) deel viii, no. 6–7; (2. sect.) deel x, no. 1–6. plates (partly
fold., partly col.) 26½^{cm}. Amsterdam, J. Müller, 1904.

Amsterdam, Koninklijke akademie van wetenschappen te. . . . Verslag
van de gewone vergaderingen der wis-en natuurkundige afdeeling van 19 december 1903
tot 23 april 1904. deel xii (1.–2. gedeelte) illus., plates (partly fold., partly col.)
26½^{cm}. Amsterdam, J. Müller, 1904.

Archiv für naturgeschichte. Gegründet von A. F. A. Wiegmann . . . 'hrsg. von
Prof. Dr. W. Weltner. 62. jahrg., ii. bd., 1. hft. 24^{cm}. Berlin, Nicolaische verlags-buchhandlung 1896 [1904]

Bergens museum. Bergens museum aarbog 1904 . . . 2. hefte. illus., plates.
24^{cm}. Bergen, J. Griegs bogtrykkeri, 1904.

Béziers, Société d'étude des sciences naturelles de. Bulletin . . . xxv.
vol.; année 1902. 25^{cm}. Béziers, H. Azais, 1903.

Boston society of natural history. By-laws . . . with a list of officers and
members. 32 p. 28½^{cm}. Boston, Press of N. Sawyer & son, 1891.

—— By-laws. 7 p. 23^{cm}. [Boston, 1896]

Brooklyn institute of arts and sciences. The sixteenth year book . . . 1903–
04 . . . front., illus., plates, ports. 20^{cm}. Brooklyn, The Institute, 1904.

Budapest. Magyar nemzeti muzeum. Annales historico-naturales Musei
nationalis hungarici. vol. ii, 1904, pars 2. illus., col. pl. 26½^{cm}. Budapest, 1904.

Budapest. Magyar tudományos akadémia. Mathematikai és természettudo manyi közlemények vonatkozólag a hazai viszonyokra . . . xxviii. kötet. 2. szám . . . 24^{cm}. Budapest, 1904.

Cambridge philosophical society. Proceedings . . . vol. xiii, pt. 1. illus. 22½^{cm}. Cambridge, University press, 1905.

Carnegie institution, *Washington, D. C.* . . . Year book, no. 3; 1904. 25^{cm}. Washington, The institution, 1905.

Danske (Kongelig) videnskabernes selskab. . : . Skrifter, 7. række, naturvidensk. og mathem. afd. i, 1–3; ii, 2–3. illus., plates (1 fold.) map. 27^{cm}. København, B. Lunos bogtrykkeri, 1904.

Davenport academy of sciences. Proceedings . . . vol. ix; 1901–03. front. (port.) xxi pl., fold. tab. 25^{cm}. Davenport, Iowa, 1904.

Freiburg i Br. (Germany) **Naturforschende gesellschaft.** . . . Berichte . . . hrsg. von Dr. K. Gerhardt. 14. bd. illus., ix pl. (partly fold., partly col.) 24^{cm}. Freiburg i. Br., C. A. Wagners universitäts-buchdruckerei, 1904.

Geneva. Société de physique et d'histoire naturelle de Genève. Mémoires . . . v. 34, fasc. 5, février 1905. illus., plates (1 double) 31^{cm}. Genève, Georg & cie. [etc., etc.] 1905.

Giornale di scienze naturali ed economiche; pubblicato per cura della Società di scienze naturali ed economiche di Palermo (vol. xxiv—anno 1904) xxix pl. 31½^{cm}. Palermo, Tipografia D. Vena, 1904.

Görlitz, Naturforschende gesellschaft zu. Abhandlungen . . . 24. bd. map. 24½^{cm}. Görlitz, H. Tzschaschel, 1904.

Hamilton scientific association. Journal and proceedings . . . for session of 1903/04. no. xx. front., ports., plates. 22^{cm}. [Hamilton] Printed for the Hamilton association by the Times printing co., 1904.

Harvard college—*Museum of comparative zoology.* Annual report . . . to the president and fellows of Harvard college for 1903–04. 23^{cm}. Cambridge, University press, 1904.

Heidelberg. Naturhistorisch-medizinischer verein. Verhandlungen . . . neue folge, 8. bd. ; 1 hft. iii pl. 24½^{cm}. Heidelberg, C. Winter's universitätsbuchhandlung, 1904.

Indian museum, *Calcutta.* . . . Annual report. April, 1901, to March, 1902. 20½^{cm}. Calcutta, The trustees, 1903.

Indian museum, *Calcutta—Industrial section.* Annual report . . . for . . . 1895/96–1900/01. 21–21½^{cm}. Calcutta, Bengal secretariat press, 1896–1901.

Jahrbuch der Hamburgischen wissenschaftlichen anstalten. xxi. jahrg.; 1903. illus., fold. tab., diagrs. 25½^{cm}. Hamburg, L. Gräfe & Sillem, 1904.

—— 1. 3. beiheft . . . 1903. illus., plates (partly double, partly fold) 25½–33½^{cm}. Hamburg, L. Grafe & Sillem, 1904.

Karlsruhe, Naturwissenschaftlicher verein in. Verhandlungen . . . 17. bd.; 1903–04. plates. 23½^{cm}. Karlsruhe, Druck der G. Braun'schen hofbuchdruckerei, 1904.

Liverpool, Literary and philosophical society of. Proceedings . . . during the 92d session, 1902–03, and the 93d session, 1903–04. no. lvii. 21½^{cm}. London, Longmans, Green & co.; [etc., etc.], 1904.

Lübeck, Geographische gesellschaft in. Mitteilungen der Geographischen-gesellschaft und des Naturhistorischen museums in Lübeck. Hrsg. vom Redaktionsausschuss. 2. reihe, hft. 19. xi pl. (1 fold.) fold. map. 26^{cm}. Lübeck, Lübcke & Nöhring, 1904.

Magdeburg, Naturwissenschaftlicher verein in. Jahresbericht und abhandlungen . . . 1902–04. 22ᶜᵐ. Magdeburg, Druck: Faber'sche buchdruckerei, 1904.

Michigan academy of science. Third, fourth, sixth report . . . 1901–02, 1904. 23ᶜᵐ. Lansing, R. Smith printing co., state printers and binders, 1902–04.

Nassauischer verein für naturkunde. Jahrbücher . . . Hrsg. von Dr. Arnold Pagenstecher . . . jahrg. 57. ii col. pl. 23ᶜᵐ. Wiesbaden, J. F. Bergmann, 1904.

Naturhistoricher verein der preussischen Rheinlande, Westfalens und des reg.-bezirks Osnabrück. Verhandlungen . . . 61. jahrg., 1904, 1. hälfte. illus., 4 pl. (1 fold.) 22ᶜᵐ. Bonn, F. Cohen, 1904.

Naturwissenschaftlicher verein für Schwaben und Neuburg. Sechsunddreissigster bericht . . . plates (partly fold.) 22½ᶜᵐ. Augsburg, Druck von P. J. Pfeiffer, 1904.

New York (*state*)—*Museum.* . . . 56th annual report, 1902. vol. 4. plates (partly col.) 23ᶜᵐ. Albany, University of the state of New York, 1904.

New York (*state*)—*Museum.* . . . Bulletin 78, archeology 9. A history of the New York Iroquois now commonly called the six nations, by William M. Beauchamp . . . 17 pl., fold. map in pocket. 23ᶜᵐ. Albany, New York state education dept., 1904.

Niederrheinische gesellschaft für natur-und heilkunde zu Bonn. Sitzungsberichte . . . 1904. 1. hälfte. 2 pl. 22ᶜᵐ. Bonn, F. Cohen, 1904.

Riga, *Russia.* **Naturforscher-verein.** Korrespondenzblatt . . . xlvii. 22½ᶜᵐ. Riga, Druck von W. F. Häcker, 1904.

Royal philosophical society of Glasgow. Proceedings . . . vol. xxxv; 1903/04. illus., 4 pl., iii diagr. (1 fold.) 23ᶜᵐ. Glasgow, The Society, 1904.

Royal society of South Australia. Transactions and proceedings and report . . . vol. xxviii. xliii pl. (partly fold., partly col.) fold. plan. 22ᶜᵐ. Adelaide, W. C. Rigby, 1904.

Senckenbergische naturforschende gesellschaft in Frankfurt am Main. Bericht . . . 1904. vom juni 1903 bis juni 1904. front., illus., v pl. (2 double) 24ᶜᵐ. Frankfurt a. M. [Druck von Gebrüder Knauer] 1904.

Sociedad científica Argentina. Anales . . . tomo vii–xx; 1879–85. plates (partly fold.) 25ᶜᵐ. Buenos Aires, Imprenta de P. E. Coni, 1879–85.

Sociedade scientifica de São Paulo. . . . Relatorio da directoria 1903–04. 23ᶜᵐ. São Paulo, Typografia Brazil de C. Gerke, 1904.

Société linnéenne de Normandie. Bulletin . . . 5. sér., 7. v; année 1903. 22½ᶜᵐ. Caen. E. Lanier, imprimeur, 1904.

Solothurn (*Switzerland*) **Naturforschende gesellschaft.** Mitteilungen . . 2. hft. (xiv. bericht) 1902–04. fold. col. pl., fold. tab. 23ᶜᵐ. Solothurn. Buchdruckerei C. Gassmann, 1904.

South Australia—*Public library, museum, and art gallery, Board of governors of the.* Report . . . for 1903–4. plates. 33½ᶜᵐ. Adelaide, C. E. Bristow, government printer, 1904.

The Sportsman, July 2–Dec. 31, 1904. v. 7. illus. 40ᶜᵐ. St. Louis and New York, Sportsman publishing co. [1904]

Svenska (Kongliga) vetenskaps-akademien. . . . Handlingar. bandet 38, n:o 4–5. 4 pl., 2 fold. diagr. 31½ᶜᵐ. Stockholm, P. A. Norstedt & söner, 1904.

Tromsø museum. . . . Aarsberetning for 1901–03. 22½ᶜᵐ. Tromsø, J. Kjeldseths bogtrykkeri, 1904.

Tromsø museum. . . . Aarshefter. 26; 1903. ix pl. 22½ᶜᵐ. Tromsø, Tromsøpostens bogtr.; 1904.

Vienna. Verein zur verbreitung naturwissenchaftlicher kenntnisse in Wien. Schriften . . . 21.-30., 32.-44. bd.; vereinsjahr 1880/81-1889/90, 1891/92-1903/04. illus., plates, maps. 19^{cm}. Wien, Im selbstverlage des vereines zur ver-breitung naturwissenschaftlicher kenntnisse in Wien, 1881-1904.

Added t.-p.: Populäre vorträge aus alien fächern der naturwissenschaft.

Wisconsin academy of sciences, arts, and letters. Transactions . . . vol. xiv, pt. ii; 1903. plates (1 fold.) ports. 25^{cm}. Madison, Democrat printing co., state printer, 1904.

Pt. 2 completes the vol.

Wisconsin state historical society. Index to the Proceedings . . . 1874-1901, prepared under the editorial direction of Reuben Gold Thwaites . . . by Mary Eliza-beth Haines. 399 p. 23^{cm}. Madison, The Society, 1904.

Zeeuwsch genootschap der wetenschappen. Archief. Vroegere en latere mededeelingen voornamelijk in betrekking tot Zeeland . . . 1904. plans (3 fold.) 23½^{cm}. Middelburg, J. C. & W. Altorffer, 1904.

Zürich, Naturforschende gesellschaft in. Neujahrsblatt . . . 1799-1895, 1902-04. 1.-97., 104.-106. stück. plates, ports., maps. 21½-28^{cm}. Zürich, In kom-mission bei Fäsi & Beer [1799-1904]

Stück 13, 68, 91, 93-95, 102-103 wanting.

1799-1870 title reads: An die zürcherische jugend . . . von der Naturforschenden gesellschaft.

Zürich, Naturforschende gesellschaft in. Vierteljahrsschrift . . . 49. jahrg.; 1904. illus., viii pl. (1 fold., 1 double). 24^{cm}. Zürich, Fäsi & Beer, 1904.

32. REFERENCE BOOKS, BIBLIOGRAPHY AND LIBRARY ECONOMY.

Almanach de Gotha. Annuaire généalogique, diplomatique et statistique 1904. 141. année. front., ports. 15^{cm}. Gotha, J. Perthes [n. d.]

American brewers' review. American brewing trade list and internal revenue guide for brewers. 1905. Supplement to the American brewers' review. 14½^{cm}. Chicago, American brewers' company [1905]

Baltimore sun. Almanac for 1904 . . . 19^{cm}. [Baltimore] From the press of the Sun book and job printing office [1904]

Boston—Public library. Annual list of new and important books added to the Public library . . . selected from the monthly bulletins 1903-04. 25½^{cm}. Boston, Published by the trustees, 1905.

Boyd's directory of the District of Columbia, 1905. 24^{cm}. Washington, The Boyd directory co., 1905.

Bullinger, Edwin Wilson, comp. Bullinger's postal and shippers' guide for the United States and Canada . . . Ed. of January 1905 . . . 984 p. 25½^{cm}. New York, E. W. Bullinger [1905]

Cercle d'études des agronomes de l'état et des membres du personnel enseignant agricole. . . . Bibliographie agricole belge. 1. ptie. 24^{cm}. Ixelles-Bruxelles, Impr. J. Vandervorst, 1904. (Cercle d'études des agronomes de l'état et des membres du personnel enseignant agricole. Publications ii)

Chicago—Public library. Thirty-second annual report of the Board of directors . . . June 1904. pl. 23^{cm}. Chicago, The Chicago public library, 1904.

Cram's standard American railway system atlas of the world . . . Accompanied by a complete and simple index of the United States. Showing the true location of all railroads, towns, villages, and post-offices . . . 496, [30] p. maps. 47½^{cm}. New York, G. F. Cram, 1905.

District of Columbia—Public library. Seventh annual report of the Board of trustees and sixth annual report of the librarian . . . for the fiscal year ended June 30, 1904. front., plates. 23^{cm}. Washington, 1904.

Harvard university—*Library.* Seventh report of William Coolidge Lane, librarian of Harvard university. 1904 . . . 23½ᶜᵐ. [n. p., n. d.]
Reprinted from the report of the president of Harvard university for 1903-04.

Hendricks' commercial register of the United States. For buyers and sellers, especially devoted to the interests of the agricultural, mechanical, engineering, contracting, electrical railroad, iron, steel, mining, mill, quarrying, and kindred industries . . . 14th annual ed. 1 p. l., XLVI, 1279 p. 26½ᶜᵐ. New York, S. E. Hendricks co., 1905.

India—*Superintendent of government printing.* List of non-confidential publications exempted from registration, which were issued by the departments of the government of India and by local governments and administrations, during the year ending 31st December, 1903. 33ᶜᵐ. [n. p., 1904]

Institut international de bibliographie, *Brussels.* . . . Classification bibliographique décimale. Tables générales refondues établies en vue de la publication du Répertoire bibliographique universel. Éd. française pub. avec le concours du Bureau bibliographique de Paris. fasc. no. 2ᵃ, 21–30. 25ᶜᵐ. Bruxelles [etc.] Institut international de bibliographie, 1904. (Institut international de bibliographie. Publication no. 25)

International catalogue of scientific literature. 2nd annual issue. D. chemistry. 21½ᶜᵐ. London, Royal society of London, 1904.

John Crerar library, *Chicago.* . . . A list of cyclopedias and dictionaries, with a list of directories. August, 1904. vi, 272 p. 27½ᶜᵐ. Chicago, Printed by order of the board of directors, 1904.

Kolonial-wirtschaftliches komitee. Kolonial-handels-adressbuch, 1905 (9. jahrg.) fold. map. 25ᶜᵐ. Berlin [1905]

New York (*state*)—*Library.* . . . 86th annual report, 1903 . . . 23ᶜᵐ. Albany, University of the state of New York, 1904.

New York (*state*)—*Library.* . . . State library bulletin 88. Bibliography 37. A selection from the best books of 1903, with notes. 23ᶜᵐ. Albany, New York state education dept., 1904.

Paris. Bibliothèque nationale. . . . Catalogue général des livres imprimés de la Bibliothèque nationale; auteurs. tome XVIII–XX. Bouron-Budzyński. 25ᶜᵐ. Paris, Imprimerie nationale, 1904.

Poor, Henry William. Poor's directory of railway officials (steam, electric, and other) containing lists of the officials of all the railroads in operation in the United States, Canada, and Mexico. Ed. of January, 1905 . . . 19th annual compilation. 22½ᶜᵐ. New York, Poor's railroad manual co. [1905]
A supplement to Poor's manual of railroads.

Poor, Henry William. Poor's ready reference bond list (ed. of January, 1905) containing all important facts required by investors, bond experts, bankers, and others relative to the bonded indebtedness, interest charges, etc., of the leading railroad systems in the United States . . . 5th annual compilation. 22ᶜᵐ. New York, Poor's Railroad manual co. [1905]
A supplement to Poor's manual of railroads.

Providence athenæum. Sixty-ninth annual report of the Board of directors . . . submitted September 26, 1904. front. 22½ᶜᵐ. [Providence.] The Providence press, Snow & Farnham, printers, 1904.

Rand, McNally & co., *pub.* . . . Enlarged business atlas and shippers' guide . . . 35th ed. xxxv, 319 p., incl. maps. 53½ᶜᵐ. Chicago, Rand, McNally & company, 1905.

Sauer, Charles Marquard. . . . Italian conversation-grammar. A new and practical method of learning the Italian language . . . 6th ed. viii, 432 p. 20^{cm}. Heidelberg, J. Groos, New York, E. Steiger & co.; [etc., etc.] 1891.

At head of title: Method Gaspey-Otto-Sauer.

The **Textile** manufacturer annual for 1905. 37½^{cm}. Manchester, Emmott and company, limited, printers [1905].

Tovey's official brewers' and malsters' directory of the United States and Canada, 1905. A supplement to the Brewers' journal . . . 14^{cm}. New York, The Brewers' journal [1904]

Vicaire, Georges. Manuel de l'amateur de livres du xixe siècle 1801–1893 . . . fasc. 15. 25^{cm}. Paris, A. Rouquette, 1904.

Completes v. 5.

Washington (*D. C.*) **academy of sciences.** Directory of the Washington academy of sciences and affiliated societies. 1903–05. 23½^{cm}. Washington, Published by the Academy, 1903–05.

Wisconsin free library commission. Fifth biennial report . . . 1903–04. 23^{cm}. Madison, Democrat printing company, state printer, 1904.

. . . **World** almanac and·encyclopedia 1905. 19½^{cm}. New York, Issued by the Press publishing co., New York World, 1904.

Year-book of the scientific and learned societies of Great Britain and Ireland; a record of the work done in science, literature, and art during the session 1903–04, by numerous societies and government institutions . . . 21st annual issue. 22½^{cm}. London, C. Griffin and company, limited, 1904.

33. RECENT ADDITIONS TO THE LIST OF PERIODICALS CURRENTLY RECEIVED.

Aberdeen and north of Scotland college of agriculture. . . . Bulletin no. 1. 21½^{cm}. Aberdeen, The Aberdeen university press, limited, 1904.

The **African** agricultural world [monthly] vol. vii, no. 11–12; Jan.–Feb., 1905. 36½^{cm}. Monrovia, Liberia, 1905.

American civic association—*Park dept.* . . . Items of park news . . . no. 2–3; Nov. 1, 1904.–Jan. 15, 1905. 23^{cm}. Hartford, The Case, Lockwood & Brainard company, 1904–05.

Anglo-Saxon stockman [monthly] vol. i no. 6, 7; Nov., 1904–Jan., 1905. illus. 35^{cm}. Toronto, 1904–05.

Annales de chimie analytique . . . année 10, tome 10, no. 1–3; Jan. 15–Mar. 15, 1905. 23^{cm}. Paris, 1905.

. . . **Annali** di botanica pubblicati dal Prof. Romualdo Pirotta . . . vol. ii, fasc. 1; Jan. 10, 1905. plates. 25½^{cm}. Roma, E. Voghera, 1905.

· The **Apteryx.** A New England quarterly of natural history [published quarterly by the Roger Williams park museum of Providence, R. I.] v. i, no. 1; Jan., 1905. plates. 23½^{cm}. Providence, 1905.

. . . **L'Avvenire** economico e le industrie del freddo . . . anno i, fascicolo 1, 3/4, 6, 7; anno. ii, fascicolo 9–11; May, July–Aug., Oct., Nov., 1904; Jan.–Mar., 1905. illus. 34^{cm}. Genova, 1904–05.

Bit & spur [monthly] vol. i, no. 1–2; March–April, 1905. illus. 31½^{cm}. Chicago, Kansas City, St. Louis, and New York, 1905.

. . . **Boys** and girls. A nature study magazine [monthly] . . . vol. iv, no. 2; Feb., 1905. illus. 23^{cm}. Ithaca, N. Y., 1904.

The **British** trade journal [monthly]   vol. XLIII, no. 505–507; Jan. 1–Mar. 1, 1905. illus. 33^{cm}. London, 1905.

The **Chemist** and Druggist [weekly]   vol. LXVI, no. 1307–1312; Feb. 11–March 18, 1905. 27½^{cm}. London, 1905.

. . . Il **Coltivatore** [weekly]   anno 51, num. 4, 10; Jan. 10, Mar. 5, 1905.   23^{cm}. Casale Monferrato, tipo-lithografia C. Cassone, 1905.

Cornell university—*College of agriculture.* . Cornell reading course for farmers' wives . . . series I–III (no. 1–13); Nov. 1902–Jan. 1905. illus. 23^{cm}. Ithaca, 1902–05.
Wanting No. 9, 10.

"**Dixie**" a monthly journal devoted to the technical features of sawmilling and woodworking. v. 20, no. 12–v. 21, no. 3; Dec., 1904–March, 1905. illus. 31½^{cm}. Atlanta, 1904–05.

L'Échange. Revue linnéenne . . . organe mensuel des naturalistes de la région lyonnaise et du centre . . . 21. année, no. 242–243; Feb.–Mar., 1905. 27½^{cm}. Moulins, 1905.

Edinburgh and east of Scotland college of agriculture. Bulletin I–IV. 22½^{cm}. Edinburgh, 1903–04.

The **Farm** star [semi-monthly]   vol. 3, no. 1; March 4, 1905. illus. 36^{cm}. Indianapolis, 1905.

. . . The **Farmer's** co-operative banner . . . [monthly]   vol. II, no. 15–16, Dec., 1904–Jan., 1905. 26½^{cm}. Hitchin, 1904–05.

. . . The **Garden** magazine [monthly]   [v. 1] no. 1–3; Feb.–Apr., 1905. illus. 21^{cm}. New York, Doubleday, Page & co., 1905.

Harper-Adams agricultural college, *Newport, Shropshire, Eng.* Bulletin no. 1–2. 22½^{cm}. [Newport] 1904.

Jornal dos agricultores. Orgão dos interesses dos lavradores do Brasil [semimonthly] anno 4, no. 16–anno 5, no. 1; Aug. 31, 1904–Jan. 15, 1905. 26½^{cm}. Rio de Janeiro, 1904.

Journal of agricultural science . . . vol. I, pt. 1; Jan., 1905. 26^{cm}. Cambridge [Eng.] 1905.

Kosmos. Naturwissenschaftliches literaturblatt und Zentralblatt für das naturwissenschaftliche bildungs- und sammelwesen herausgegeben von Kosmos, gesellschaft der naturfreunde. Stuttgart. bd. 1, hft. 1–3. 24^{cm}. Stuttgart, 1904.

The **Leather** trades' review [weekly] vol. XXXVIII, no. 981–991; Jan. 4–March 15, 1905. 28^{cm}. London, 1905

Maine sportsman. v. 12, no. 136–139; Dec. 1904–March, 1905. illus. 29½^{cm}. Bangor, 1904–05.

Milchwirtschaftliches zentralblatt. (Wissenchaftliche monatsbeilage der Milchzeitung) . . . 1.'jahrg., hft. 1–3; Jan.–March, 1905. 23½^{cm}. Leipzig, 1905.

Le **Moniteur** du caoutchouc et des autres gommes lacticifères, commerce, industrie, cultures . . . [monthly] 2. année, no. 15; Jan., 1905. illus. 32½^{cm}. Bruxelles, 1905.

The **National** coopers' journal . . . [monthly] vol. XX, no. 9–11; Jan.–March, 1905. illus. 39^{cm}. Philadelphia, 1905.

The **Nature-study** review. vol. I, no. 1–2; Jan.–March, 1905. illus. 23½^{cm}. Lancaster, Pa., and New York City, 1905.

The **Naval** stores review and journal of trade [weekly]. vol. XIV, no. 42–52; Jan. 14–Mar. 25, 1905. 28^{cm}. Savannah, 1905.

Pacific fancier . . . [monthly]. vol. I, no. 1, Feb., 1905. illus. 31ᶜᵐ. Los Angeles, 1905.

Le **Progrès** vétérinaire. Journal de médecine bovine . . . [semi-monthly]. 18. année, nouv. sér., no. 1–4; Jan. 10–Feb. 25, 1905. 22ᶜᵐ. Agen, 1905.

Pure products, published monthly by the Scientific station for pure products. vol. I, no. 1–3; Jan.–March, 1905. 25½ᶜᵐ. New York, 1905.

Revista vitivinícola argentina . . . [semi-monthly]. año 1, núm. 2, 7; Nov. 25, 1904; Feb. 10, 1905. 27½ᶜᵐ. Mendoza, 1904–05.

Shields' magazine . . . vol. I, no. 1; March, 1905. illus. 24ᶜᵐ. New York, G. O. Shields, 1905.

Skogsvårdsföreningens tidskrift . . . utgifven af föreningen för skogsvård. 2. årg., 12. häftet—3. årg., 2. häftet; Dec., 1904–Feb., 1905. illus. maps. 25½ᶜᵐ. Stockholm, 1904–05.

The **Southern** field. Devoted to the agricultural, manufacturing, mining, and business interests of the country tributary to the Southern railway. vol. 10, no. 1–2; Jan.–March, 1905. illus. 37½ᶜᵐ. Washington, 1905.

Süddeutsche tabakzeitung. Fachwissenschaftliches und -handelspolitisches zentralorgan für die tabak- und cigarrenfabrikation den tabakbau und tabakhandel [semi-weekly] 15. jahrg., nr. 1–22; Jan. 1–Mar. 14, 1905. 46ᶜᵐ. Mannheim, 1905.

Texas field and sportsman, Feb., 1902–Jan., 1904. v. 1–2. illus., plates. 23½ᶜᵐ. San Antonio, 1902–04.

Die **Umschau**, übersicht über die fortschritte und bewegungen auf dem gesamtgebiet der wissenschaft, technik, literatur und kunst [weekly] IX. jahrg., no. 1–12; Jan. 1–Mar. 18, 1905. illus. 29ᶜᵐ. Frankfurt, H. Bechhold, 1905.

The **Veterinary** record . . . [weekly] vol. XVII, no. 861–870; Jan. 5–March 11, 1905. 27½ᶜᵐ. London, 1905.

Wochenschrift für brauerei. Eigentum des Vereins versuchs- und lehranstalt für brauerei in Berlin . . . XXII. jahrg., nr. 1–10; Jan. 7–March 11, 1905. illus. 33ᶜᵐ. Berlin, P. Parey, 1905.

Zeitschrift für experimentelle pathologie und therapie . . . 1. bd., 1.–2. hft. illus. plates. 26½ᶜᵐ. Berlin, A. Hirschwald, 1905.

Zeitschrift für zuckerindustrie in Böhmen. jahrg. XXIX, hft. 1–5; Oct., 1904–Feb., 1905. 26ᶜᵐ. Prag, 1904–05.

. . . **Zemlioradnichka** zadruga. (La coopération rurale) Organ glavnoga saveza srpskikh zemlioradnichkikh zadruga [semi-monthly] vol. X, no. 1—vol. XI, no. 4; Jan. 15, 1904–Feb. 28, 1905. 33½ᶜᵐ. Beograd, 1904–05.

O